Canadian Real Estate Investing Lessons "From the Streets"

How You Can Sort Through All the Real Estate Information Available and Implement the Key Components for Maximum Success.

Authors:
Tom Karadza
Nick Karadza

Tom Karadza and Nick Karadza are licensed Real Estate Brokers in Ontario, Canada. Tom Karadza and Nick Karadza are not licensed attorneys, lawyers, tax advisors, accountants, or any other licensed professionals. **_Anyone considering implementing these ideas and plans are advised to seek professional advice concerning legal and tax matters_**.

Copyright © 2009 Karadza Publishing Inc.

No part of this book may be reproduced, stored in a retrieval system, or transmitted by any means without the written permission of the author and co-author.

ISBN: 978-1-4276-4287-5

Printed in Canada

We dedicate this book to all the investors we have worked with over the years.

It is the experiences that we go through together that help us all continue to grow.

- Tom & Nick Karadza

Introduction

When we started looking into investing in real estate we quickly realized that there was an abundance of information available from a wide variety of sources.

One of our toughest challenges was sifting through it all to determine what applied to us here in Canada because so much material was based on American laws.

An even bigger obstacle was actually implementing the information. We found out that there were many people willing to stand in front of a room and speak about some real estate investing concepts, but implementing them in the real world brought on a whole new set of challenges.

This book was conceived by facing these challenges head on and learning from first hand experience. The lessons shared in these pages were learned the hard way – by battling through our fears and taking action "on the streets"

Use the short lessons, stories and rants in this book to help leap frog your over any investing challenges you may be facing right now.

Make your journey a fun one.

We invest to live our lives on our terms, and wish you the same!

To Your Success,

Tom & Nick Karadza

Table of Contents

1. Real Estate Investing Guide "Step-by-Step" and in Plain English...1

2. Finally, A Quick Guide To Investment Property Mortgages..........14

3. Residential Real Estate Investing "Explained in Plain English!" ..25

4. Financing Investment Properties – 3 Often Overlooked "Gotchas"... 31

5. "To Get Rich in Real Estate Investing Know The Difference Between How The Pros and The Amateurs Behave"…............34

6. What does Mountain Biking at Blue Mountain have to do with Real Estate Investing in Canada?...................................43

7. "When Buying Rental Properties The Velocity of Money is Key!" 47

8. Rental Property Investing With "Nice Homes in Nice Areas" 52

9. "Real Estate Investing for Beginners Means Keeping The Proper Perspective" 56

10. Forget Motivated Sellersind Nice Homes....................................59

11. The Real Estate Investing Basics Of Single Family Rental Properties 61

12. Learn About Real Estate Investing Using Student Rental Properties 66

13. Real Estate Investing Strategy "Be An Active Investor, Not A Passive One" 70

14. "Cash Flow Is A Mystery for Canadian Real Estate Investing Beginners"...73

i

15. "The Top 10 Mistakes Made On A Canadian Real Estate Investment" 82

16. Canadian Real Estate Investments: Real Stories From "The Streets" 86

17. Canadian Real Estate Trends Are More Important Than "The Numbers" 94

18. Knowing Your Credit Score Is Critical When Real Estate Investing 100

19. Canadian Real Estate Investing Experts - The 3 Types That Can Make or Break You 103

20. Valuable Lessons Can be Taken from EVERY Experience 107

21. "Real Estate Investing Secrets That Are Convenient To Ignore" 110

22. The 5 W's of Real Estate Investing Clubs 114

23. Buying Investment Real Estate Requires The Proper Mindset .. 118

24. "Your Education In Real Estate Investing Must Include Fire Fighting...And Yes, We're Serious!" 122

25. A Real Estate Investing Program Works *IF* You Don't Quit Like Everyone Else 125

26. Real Estate Investment Book "Income For Life for Canadians" And a BIG LESSON! 129

27. Investing In Commercial Real Estate - Is The Grass Always Greener? Maybe. 132

28. The Top 10 Real Estate Investing FAQ List - Part 1 136

29. "Creative Real Estate Investing May Be Bad For Your Long Term Success" 144

30. Advice For Canadian Real Estate Investors From George Ross 148

31. "Your Investment In Rental Property Should Include This Line of Thinking" 152

32. "Attention All Canadian Real Estate Websites, Blogs, Posts & Everyone Else - We Have News For You....Your House is NOT an Asset!" 155

33. "Real Life Real Estate Investing May Require You To Get Upset - A Lot" 159

34. Canadian Real Estate Foreclosures & "The Hype" 164

35. "Toronto Rental Properties Won't Make You Rich - But The Process of Aquiring Them Will!" 168

36. Rental Real Estate Investing - Some Financing Tips to Consider Before You Make YourMove 172

37. "Real Estate Investing Opportunities Can Create Lifetime Value For You" 176

38. Your Real Estate Investment Business Plan 181

39. A Real Estate Investing Club Is Only As Good As The People In It 187

40. Real Estate Investing Courses Have Some Critical Numbers You Should Focus On 191

41. Real Estate Investing Education. You Need To Get Good At "Macro" and "Micro" 194

42. Real Estate Investment in Canada. The Power of "Set It Forget It" 197

43. Mr. B & The Status Quo 202

44. Real Estate Investing Programs With "Two Monks Lost in Communist Corporate Canada" 205

45. Let's End The Whole "Knowledge is Power" Debate 209

46. Special Gift From Tom & Nick # 1 213

47. Special Gift From Tom & Nick # 2 214

48. Special Gift From Tom & Nick # 3 215

49. Contact the Authors 216

50. About the Authors 217

1
Real Estate Investing Guide "Step-by-Step" and in Plain English

Use this real estate investing guide and you will save years (yes, years!) of wasted effort. The goal of this real estate investing guide is to give you **useful information in a step-by-step process**. Please understand that these are our opinions and are based on actual "real world" experiences with our clients.

Ready? Let's go...

Why Are You Going to Begin Real Estate Investing?

Usually you're so excited at the thought of making "Donald Trump like money" that you may not sit down and actually determine *why* you are investing in real estate.

Even **"The Donald"** has his reasons, and so should you. By deciding why you are investing from the beginning, it will help guide your education and your **decision making**.

Are you interested in monthly "cash flow"?

Are you looking for a big pay day after a few months? A few years?

Are you looking to build an asset base that creates passive income for you while you're sipping cold drinks on the beach?

Are you looking for "hands off" investing or "active" investing?

All set?

Great stuff! **Be sure to keep this in mind** while you go through the rest of the real estate investing guide.

Real Estate Investing Guide Step #1
Education - Get Some!

Now, this first step is where most people immediately go off in the wrong direction.

There are HUGE differences in the **types and levels** of real estate investing training available.

This is a case where you really want to work by **referral**. Begin asking people who are successful investors how they started, what real estate education they used, what real estate books they read, and what mentors they had.

Ask them this: **"Is anyone DOING any investing who has taken the training that they're recommending?"** I often see people spend more time talking about investing and more time posting about investing in discussion forums than actually spend DOING anything.

So when you ask around, look for an **active group** that is actually doing real world investing and not just sitting in a class or banquet hall all day.

ASIDE: Let me make something clear right now: Driving to a "real estate investment meeting" once a month does not make you money. You need to get out of your comfort zone and actually do something. Keep reading so that you discover why a SYSTEM is key to your success.

A mistake made by many people is asking your neighbor or cousin or father-in-law about investing. Unless one of these people is successfully doing it, be very careful about taking their advice.

Many, MANY, people make the mistake of taking advice from people that have no business in giving it. **Don't let that be you.**

Agreed? Good, let's move on.

"Flipping" is Very Different from "Investing" in Real Estate

When I began my journey in investing, there was no real estate investing guide to break down what is now a very simple, **yet incredibly important** concept.

Here it is...

There is a huge difference in Real Estate **"Flipping"** or "Rehabbing" and **"Investing"**.

Flipping a house (or Rehabbing a house) the way you see it done on the many A&E TV shows looks exciting, but there are more than a few dangers to this approach.

To "flip" a house, you typically need to buy it well below market value. **This can be extremely difficult to do consistently**. Trying to find a property that you can lock up substantially below market value will take a great deal of effort.

You will need to either:

a.) Find a realtor willing to make a lot of offers on your behalf.

Also, understand that realtors work with other realtors. It's a network. If they submit 100 **low ball offers** on houses for you, they run the risk of upsetting the network that they depend on to make a living. So it can be extremely difficult to have a realtor work with you like this. Impossible? No. Difficult? **Yes!**

OR

b.) Write a lot of offers on homes yourself.

Now, to do this, you really need to get some detailed advice on what clauses to use in your offers and exactly what type of offers to write. You may want to negotiate an "option" on a property instead of buying it outright.

Regardless, before writing **any offer** on a property yourself, you will want to know what "comparable" properties in the area sold for recently. This way, you better understand the local market.

ASIDE: Real estate is a "local" game. Anyone who believes the media headlines as to whether the entire real estate market is UP or DOWN is a rookie. There are areas of the country where real estate is appreciating in a "perceived" down market. And there are areas where real estate can be losing value, while the majority of the market is increasing in value.

Writing offers on many properties will be necessary to find someone willing to sell you their property for well below market value.

And to make money on a property you must purchase it for **substantially less than market value**. Even if the property is in good condition and requires little or no work, you have expenses that quickly chew up any potential profits.

Things like advertising, real estate commissions (if you use a realtor to sell the property after you buy it), legal costs on closing, **land transfer taxes**, and taxes on your profits will eat into your profits extremely quickly.

A "Deal" is a "Deal" for a Reason.
Make Sure You Know What That Reason Is!

Often the real reason you are able to get a house for below market value is because the house is in **below average condition**. Sometimes, well below.

Remember, there's a reason you're getting a "deal".

This isn't necessarily a problem, it could be an **opportunity**, just be aware of it. This obvious point is regularly overlooked.

It is possible to get a home that doesn't need much or any work at all. It just takes a LONG time to track one of those down. See points **a)** and **b)** above about writing offers.

Flipping Can Create Lumps of Money, Investing Should Create Cash Flow

Typically, you invest for cash flow. Or, if you are not receiving cash flow, you are getting tax incentives, an equity increase or appreciation. **Usually, cash flow is king.**

Now, when you are flipping a house, you typically have cash flowing in one direction...out of your hands.

Things like renovations, mortgage payments, **unexpected permits**, delays, advertising and commissions all cost you money. You spend all this money with the hopes of a pay day at the end of it.

I call this "speculation". You are **speculating** that someone will pay you more for your property than you paid for it.

When you are **investing**, you are looking to invest "into demand". There's a huge reason for this.

When you invest into a property that is in demand, you can start having cash flow INTO your hands shortly after (or sometimes even before) you own the property. It's a much more civilized way to deal with Real Estate.

Ask around -- you'll uncover stories of people trying to flip real estate who lose the property after dumping tens of thousands of dollars into it. Or, if they do manage to sell their flip, the lump of profit at the end is often much less than anticipated.

Please don't misunderstand me. You can make BIG money flipping properties. You just need a BIG bankroll to do it or a partner who has one. The risk when flipping, as opposed to investing, is greater.

Investing in real estate typically means purchasing an income producing asset that is currently or can quickly generate cash flow for you.

There are many opportunities to buy properties and quickly increase the existing cash flow. Or to buy properties that have no existing cash flow, but are in such demand that they can be quickly turned into income generators with minimal effort.

So there you have it. The difference between flipping and investing is **cash flow**....namely, the direction of it!

Personally, flipping a house is like creating a job for yourself. There's a **ton of work** for you to do yourself or manage.

Also, flipping is difficult to reproduce. It can be challenging to systematically find properties that are below value. So, you may hit a gem **once** and then go through long periods of time with nothing.

Investing in real estate is creating cash flow for yourself.

And typically, with a good system, you can invest in properties that produce cash flow **regularly and consistently**.

You can make money at both, just go into each knowing the difference.

The differences between flipping and investing are often not covered in detail in various real estate education material.

A collection of cash flow producing real estate investments can create financial independence.

Flipping homes is more like **creating a job for yourself**. If you take the income and invest it into cash flow properties, it can really accelerate the growth of your asset base.

Each has its place, know the difference.

Here's our **Real Estate Investment Guide** Step 1 Summary:

Decide what you want from your real estate investing: lump sums of money or constant passive income. This is key in helping you decide which moves to make.

Work by referral to uncover local groups of ACTIVE investors. If that group will not train you directly, ask them where they went as beginners.

Don't get caught up in investment groups that spend all day in training classes or on discussion forums and don't actually DO anything.

Learn different real estate strategies and the terminology, e.g. flipping vs. investing.

Real Estate Investing Guide Step #2
Mentors - Find One!

The people around you are critical to your success in anything, not just real estate investing.

If you don't have access to someone who has done or is doing real estate investing, **start looking now**.

You will be infinitely better off by having someone that you can bounce ideas off of and run your decisions by.

I'll regularly run into people who take some real estate training and then run into the real world without any more guidance. Typically, these people will run into all the **regular roadblocks and won't have anyone to help navigate them**.

A mentor can share stories with you, teach you about structuring deals, teach you about cash flow, steer you clear of mortgage financing issues and ultimately save you from yourself.

If you don't have a mentor and can't find one immediately, you have a couple of options.

Firstly, read, read, read. Read everything you can about real estate investing. Learn from other people. The authors of good books can be your "virtual" mentors. For years they were mine.

Start Creating Your Power Team Immediately

Secondly, start making relationships with a group of people that together make up **your team of experts**. Each person will have some knowledge for you, and together, they can be a powerful group.

For example, a good mortgage broker who really understands investment mortgages can be a **savior**.

A real estate lawyer who **understands** things like detailed lease agreements may be worth his/her weight in gold when you are structuring a contract.

An accountant who can **save you money and protect** your wealth is invaluable.

An advertising rep at the local newspaper who can place your ads in the paper quickly can be **worth thousands**.

A good insurance broker can save you hundreds of dollars a year in premiums and provide **maximum liability protection** at the same time.

Together, these people can become a very powerful point of leverage for you.

They are your POWER TEAM.

Here's something that WILL occur. One day, you will be making an investment and you will hit some sort of snag.

Maybe it's that the bank doesn't like the way you structured the offer to purchase, or maybe the lawyer doesn't think they can close a deal for you **fast enough**.

When these things happen you need a second choice. You need to be able to **ring up** someone else really quickly to verify that what you are hearing is correct.

The Worst Number When Creating Your Team is "One"

Never have one contact, **never**.

Too many people hear "no" from one source and accept it as fact. That's a sure way never to get anything done.

A good mentor or a **team of good professionals** will definitely save you time and most always save you money. It's never too early or too late to start building a team of good contacts.

Be **careful** not to burn these people as well. It's a small world, and if you tell someone who has the ability to help you that you are going to do something....do it.

Otherwise, you will quickly fall out of favour with them.

If you are going to be taken seriously then take yourself seriously. **Your word should be law**.

Don't burn bridges.

When people begin to notice that you actually do what you say you will do you are going to stand apart from the crowd. People will be drawn to you.

Let's wrap up this section with a little **tip**.

Instead of taking years to create this powerful team around you, find someone that is an active investor and ask them who they use.

Likely, they have spent a long time assembling people they trust. So infiltrate their network if possible. Don't be overly aggressive, just ask permission and then **charge ahead**.

Real Estate Investing Guide Step #3
A System - Use One!

This is by FAR the most important part of real estate investing and it is **by FAR the most overlooked**.

Here are some very common scenarios:

1. You take some real estate training. Or, you buy some books on real estate investing. Or you've **bought a course** on how to invest in real estate.

2. You finish the training/book/course with a bunch of new information on: renovating, flipping, renting, **options**, lease options, sandwich lease options, assignments, multi-units, commercial investing, cash flow investing, private money lending, **second mortgages**, discount mortgages, land development...you get the idea.

3. You run out and **like a madman** start firing in all directions.

4. You begin looking for anything and everything. You start working with anyone and everyone. You call agents, brokers, for sale by owners. Or maybe you **hit the road** and place some advertisements stating that you are looking for homes or that you buy run down properties.

5. You get a few calls. **Some excitement** builds and then within a few weeks, it all fades away.

6. You then either forget about real estate investing all together, or **limp along** like that for a long time, never getting anywhere.

Your friends think they are proven right: the whole real estate investing idea was nuts to begin with.

This approach typically **doesn't yield consistent results**. You may get lucky and get one good deal, but it will be difficult to consistently create another one.

Every successful real estate investor has a **system,** whether they know it or not.

Donald Trump may not have a binder behind his desk labeled, "The Trump System to Real Estate". But believe me -- he has a way of doing things that systematically makes him money. He goes about his deals with a strategy.

Don't **fall into the trap** of running around looking for any old property and then sending it over to your mortgage broker to see if you can qualify for it.

You're so eager to buy something, anything, that you don't fully understand what you are **getting yourself into**. You almost don't care.

I know because I see it all the time. Only AFTER you purchase the triplex is it that you realize the **rents are a "bit" low** and the condition of it really isn't that great.

Then someone moves out of one of the units and you really have **no idea** what you're doing when it comes to advertising and placing a new tenant.

Weeks, even months go by, and now your great property is costing you money instead of making you money.

Make sure you discuss **any and all** deals with your mentor or team of experts (see Step #2 above). They will keep you on track.

And remember, make sure the person you use as a mentor is **actually doing** the same type of investments or has done the exact same ones in the past.

A lot of people will take some real estate investing seminars and learn a lot but fail to **put a system in place**.

And the people that taught the seminar are likely gone or not willing to hit the streets with you and implement. Unless you implement what you have learned there is no money to be made.

You need a system.

Let's use an analogy here.

Henry Ford's Assembly Line Was a "System" That Consistently Output a Valuable Product

Imagine you took a course or read a book about tires, engines, metal and leather. You then decide that you are going to make money selling cars.

Unless you have the "system" in place, in this case the assembly line, you will likely **fall hard** trying to pull this off.

Henry Ford got really rich because he had the best system.

Not because he had the best **tires and metal**.

Why is it that people who learn a bit about real estate contracts, a bit about flipping a house, a bit about selling houses often fail?

No system.

You need to have one.

A good system covers everything throughout the entire real estate investing process

There's more to real estate investing than finding a property and locking it up.

How are you going to sell it? **Agent or no agent**? How are you going to advertise it? Where are you going to advertise it?

How many **calls can you expect**? What are you going to say when people do call? This is critical.

How are you going to fix it up? **Contractors**? You? Your cousin Frank? How are you going to place a tenant in it?

How much can you expect to get in rent? How fast can you get the rent (before your next mortgage payment)? Who is going to handle all the **tenant calls**?

Who is going to handle the small repairs? How are you going to handle property management? How are you going to strategically reduce the amount of calls you get from tenants?

How are you going to extract as much money as possible as fast as possible? Who is going to **prepare you**, in advance, for the unknown costs that WILL come up?

Who is going to steer you in the right direction when you begin to stray off course?

A good system **will answer all of these questions for you**. Spraying offers blindly all over the place is just one part of any potential system.

Too many people don't realize this and focus on writing offers without having the big picture in mind.

So, now that you know a system is a good thing, **where do you find one**?

Each successful investor will have their own. They may not refer to it as a "system" per say. It may be "the way they work", or "how they do things". But they have one. Ask for it.

It is the single most important ingredient that is missing from almost all books and all courses.

Many are teaching real estate investors to piece meal instead of going on the streets and implementing an actual system.

So remember: education, mentors and systems. When investing for maximum success you'll want all three of these. One of the pieces to the real estate investing puzzle is not enough.

2
Finally, a Quick Guide to Investment Property Mortgages

Have you ever tried to get **details** on residential investment property mortgages?

Let me tell you, it's a **real adventure**.

Your local Canadian bank branch usually doesn't have a clue and ends up scaring you off from doing any residential real estate investing all together.

There are some **excellent people** in bank branches -- you just need to find them.

Basically, bank branches aren't set up to deal with the **questions** investors have and they work on residential investment property mortgages so infrequently that they usually don't know the details.

An **experienced mortgage broker** will usually serve you better in this area.

Canadian Banks & Mortgage Brokers

Some banks don't deal with mortgage brokers. BMO isn't using them right now and RBC has their own team of **mobile mortgage representatives**.

I have experience with the Royal Bank brokers, and they have proven to be **very good**.

One thing to note when you are dealing with a bank directly is that you are **limited to the mortgage products that they offer** and sometimes you won't even know that other, better suited, options are available to you.

For example, there is a 5% down investment property mortgage program available to Canadians right now. If your bank is **not offering** the program, they may not even tell you that this exists elsewhere.

So, if you are using BMO or RBC directly, or for that matter, if you are using **any bank directly for your mortgage**, it's smart to check in with an experienced mortgage broker as well.

That way you've covered **almost** all options available to you.

I say "almost" because there are **private institutions** that will lend you money (Xceed Financial) and "**hard money**" lenders. We'll discuss this in more detail later on.

"So What Should I Know About Investment Property Mortgages?"

Know this: they are constantly changing and there are new mortgages for investment properties becoming available **almost monthly**!

So again, an experienced mortgage broker is likely your best answer.

Investment Property Mortgages: Some Background for Context

When buying an investment property, you are likely looking to put as little down as possible to gain maximum leverage.

ASIDE: Now, be aware that when you do this, if your property value falls, you could have a mortgage amount that is more than the value of your property. You really want to work with a mentor or coach who can offer some experience and guidance.

When you put **less than 20% down on a residential property** in Canada, you are using what is referred to as a "high ratio" mortgage.

ASIDE: A property is usually classified as 'residential' if it has up to **four living units**. So, mostly, single family homes up to four plexes. Anything greater is usually classified as a **commercial property** and the mortgage qualifications are very different. More on this coming up in a later chapter.

Whenever you put less than a 20% down payment, the banks use "**mortgage insurers**" to insure the mortgage. This is because of the perceived higher risk that you may default on the mortgage payments.

The **largest mortgage insurer in Canada** is CMHC, The Canadian Mortgage and Housing Corporation .

Genworth Financial Canada is another mortgage insurer and is the largest **private sector supplier** of mortgage insurance.

Now, here's where things get interesting.

CMHC has **dominated** the Canadian market for mortgage insurance since I was sucking on a baby bottle.

Well, over the last few years, Genworth, in what I believe must be an attempt to get more market share, has aggressively been offering **fantastic new mortgage insurance programs**.

One of the best was introduced in 2007. It was a **10% down payment** mortgage program for investment property mortgages. Before this, you had to put 15% down and some banks would tell you that you needed to put 25% or even 35% down. That's pretty nutty, if you ask me.

16

Well, the **lack of mortgage insurance competition** here in Canada has finally attracted some U.S. insurers.

And now, AIG has entered the market and PMI and **one other** U.S. based insurer have plans to enter into Canada as well.

All the money that CMHC has been making has finally attracted some other players.

And this leads us to our next point...

Investment Property Mortgages
-- The Mortgage Programs --

As mentioned above, until 2007 you really got a lot of **strange answers** when asking banks and brokers about investment property mortgages.

My first experiences, years ago, were down right confusing. I remember sitting in a branch of one of the big banks feeling like I had to **pull teeth to get any answers.**

I was being told I had to put down 25% for investment property mortgages. And then a few days later, I was informed they made some changes and I may actually have to put down **35%**.

Today, it's **much better**, although you're still in somewhat uncharted waters unless you have someone with experience working with you.

Here's a summary of the investment property mortgage scene.

ASIDE: Remember: the products and programs are constantly changing, so to get the most current information, work with an experienced broker or banker.

-- 20% Down Payments --
Investment Property Mortgages

If you choose to use a 20% down payment for investment property mortgages, the **world is your oyster**. Most financial institutions will bend over backwards to get your business.

You are considered **very low risk** to default on the mortgage.

You'll still need a good credit score and the income necessary to qualify for the mortgage, but overall, you are in **good shape** to shop for a mortgage anywhere you please.

You should be able to get the most attractive interest rates available, **whether** you choose to go with a fixed rate or a variable rate.

You should also be able to negotiate an 'open mortgage' -- which means that there is no mortgage penalty (often 3 months worth of interest) if you sell the house and **pay off the mortgage early**.

If you aren't able to negotiate an open mortgage then ask if your mortgage is **"portable"**. If it is, you may be able to move this mortgage into another investment property with **no penalty or reduced penalties**.

And you should be able to **avoid** having to purchase mortgage insurance all together.

Each bank and/or credit union differs on this point but with some **minimal effort and negotiation,** you should be able to avoid investment properties mortgage insurance.

These are the details that an experienced mortgage broker can help you with.

On to the fun stuff!

-- 10% Down Payments --
Investment Property Mortgages

Now things get interesting.

In **2007,** Genworth Financial began insuring investment property mortgages with 10% down payments.

This was huge. Until this was announced, you were stuck with 15% as the lowest down payment you could use.

I believe this may have been announced as a great way to attract more mortgage business from the large Canadian banks.

Also, it was announced at a time when there were rumblings that AIG (a U.S. mortgage insurer) was going to enter the Canadian market with similar offerings.

Competition is good!

This is a great program that **finally** introduced a way to purchase residential real estate (up to four units) with a 10% down payment.

There are a **few** details that your mortgage broker or banker should cover with you. One is that the **insurance premium** on this program is higher than for mortgages on a primary place of residence (a mortgage on a home that you live in).

Depending on your tax planning expertise, and, which real estate investment strategy you use, the higher premium **shouldn't be a show stopper for you**. If you want more info on the tax planning, talk to a financial planner or your accountant.

Overall, this 10% program is a **major step forward** in financing investment property mortgages. That's fantastic news for all of us investors!

-- 5% Down Payments --
Investment Property Mortgages

CMHC announced the unthinkable towards the end of 2007.

They came out with mortgage insurance for investment property mortgages with a down payment of **5% and even 0%**. Recently, the government of Canada has mandated that the 0% mortgages be halted, so a few bad apples have ruined the fun for the rest of us ;)

ASIDE:
If you are planning on purchasing multiple investment properties, you really want to speak to a mortgage broker to develop a long term plan. There are some situations where a couple of 5% down purchases can thwart your effort to buy more properties (even with more money put down).

A **few short** years ago, having a 5% down option for an investment property was unimaginable, but here we are.

With the big U.S. **players** entering the Canadian mortgage insurance market, it's my bet that CMHC is making some early moves to fight off that competition.

To gain market share, these U.S. insurers, may begin offering some more aggressive mortgage programs and CMHC is **circling the wagons to protect its turf**.

Remember, this is an opinion only, but I'm thinking I'm right on this.

Whatever the reason, Canadians now have access to 5% down payment investment property mortgages!

This is huge.

Of course, there are details to be aware of. One of them is that the insurance premium on these investment property mortgages is high, very high.

So get all the details from someone with experience dealing with these **types of products**. You may have even better alternatives.

Remember to always ask about mortgage penalties if you **pay off** the mortgage early (because you sell the property) and ask if the mortgage is portable, so that you can transfer it to another property.

Each Canadian bank is different, and not all of them will choose to offer **investment property mortgages** with these mortgage insurance options, so you will have to ask your bank to check your options.

There is **at least one** financial institution offering the program for 5% down payments.

"What Are My Other Options?"

With Genworth Financial's 10% program and CMHC's 5% program these really are the **golden years** of residential investment property mortgages in Canada.

But there are other options...

If you really want to get **aggressive** you can turn to "hard money" lenders. These are basically mortgage brokers or **other professionals** who have access to individuals willing to lend you money.

There are still qualifications to meet, but they may be less stringent. You'll **pay for this** privilege though, typical hard money loans have interest rates of 12% or higher, with finder fees tacked on to them as well.

Venture into "hard money" investment property mortgages with caution, and **work with an experienced** real estate investor/coach/mentor only.

Plus, there are **private institutions** like Xceed Financial that have offered 5% down mortgages in the past for investors without perfect credit. With recent changes in the financial industry, these may vanish soon.

However, for these types of investment property mortgages, you will require high enough income, a good to great credit score and you will likely jump through a **few extra** qualification hoops.

-- *Amortization Periods* --
Investment Property Mortgages

Canadian investment property mortgages have had recent changes around amortization periods.

Until 2006, almost all **your options** involved using a 25-year amortization period or less.

Today, we can get amortization periods on investment property mortgages all the way up to **35-year amortizations**.

There are a couple of driving forces behind these changes. With home prices **increasing** across Canada rapidly, longer appreciations allow for lower monthly payment and therefore more people can qualify for **home ownership**.

Getting people into their own homes is one of the main reasons for the existence of mortgage insurers like CMHC.

Some recent studies reported that younger Canadian families are more interested in **'lifestyle'** than **'paying off their mortgage'**.

So, with lower monthly payments as a result of longer amortization periods, the mortgage insurers are giving the **public** what it's looking for (apparently).

Longer amortization periods also mean that you are paying much more **interest** on your mortgage throughout its life. That is, each of your mortgage payments has a higher portion going to interest instead of the principle portion of the mortgage. For the home that you are purchasing to live in, this may not be the best situation.

But, for investors, long amortization periods on investment property mortgages have two main advantages:

1. The interest paid on these mortgages is tax deductible.
2. The lower monthly payment can reduce your monthly carrying costs very nicely.

Out of **everything discussed** around investment property mortgages, amortization periods get the most animated response from people.

So, if you are not sure what choices you should be making, find an experienced coach or mentor and **bounce your questions** off them.

"What Else Should I Know?"

There are details, **fine print** and exceptions to almost everything.

Things like mortgage penalties, mortgage insurance rates and mortgage **terms** need to be addressed.

So, you will need to do your homework and make sure the investment property mortgages you use are **right for you**.

Ask **questions**, don't be scared. If what the bank or mortgage broker is offering you is confusing, get clarification.

3
Residential Real Estate Investing "Explained in Plain English!"

Residential real estate investing has so many great angles and opportunities to **create wealth** that it really gets my juices flowing with excitement!

For a **beginner or even an experienced** residential real estate investor, there is a lot to learn and we're going to break out some things to think about right here.

Everyone -- and I mean everyone (your neighbour, friends, family, even **in-laws**) -- has their opinions on what is right and what isn't when it comes to real estate.

And that's what makes this such an **entertaining** (and if done right), profitable, topic.

Ready to rock? **Let's go...**

Residential Real Estate Investing
vs.
Commercial Real Estate Investing

One of the first things you should know about real estate investing is that, in general, any building that has four or more units in it is referred to as a **commercial property**. Even if those units are used for residential purposes. For example, an apartment building is a commercial property.

There are exceptions to this, but in general, that's the case.

Commercial investment properties are also things like **strip malls, office buildings, industrial units, warehouses** etc.

This is important to know, because lenders (the banks) treat these properties **very** differently when it comes to getting financing.

For commercial properties, it's much more likely you'll have to put **25% or more** as a down payment.

As we have discussed in the previous chapter, you can put as little as 5% down on residential properties.

The difference with commercial transactions is that it's much more typical to see '**vendor take backs**'.

This is where the seller carries back a portion of the value of the property (let's say 25%) and you pay a **fixed amount every month** to them, just as you would the bank.

The ability to get commercial investment properties at 0% down exists and there's definitely **more creative vendor/seller take back financing** that goes on in this arena compared to residential real estate investing.

If you use a mortgage broker for the transaction, you will also likely pay a 'broker fee'. For residential real estate investing transactions, the broker's fee is **paid by the bank** that takes the mortgage.

"What else is different with commercial versus residential real estate investing?"

The way residential properties are valued is very different from that of commercial properties.

To **value** commercial investment properties, it requires more detailed understandings of things like cash flow, cash on cash return, net operating income and return on equity.

Residential real estate investing is a **different animal** all together.

People who focus on commercial investment properties may not focus as strongly on the **factors that are important** to residential real estate investing.

Things like the importance and appreciation of the neighborhood, **comparable property prices**, financing options, the residential real estate investing purchase and sale process and finding residential tenants.

Basically, commercial properties are typically valued based on some form of income calculation, while residential real estate investing uses comparable properties to come up with a **dollar value**.

The **concepts** are similar but the expertise required is different.

-- *Residential Real Estate Investing* --
Pick an Area

There are a few key ingredients when choosing an area in which to invest.

Firstly, you'll want to decide if you prefer to have your properties close to you or not.

If you'd prefer to have **easy access** to your properties, then you will want to choose a strategy or type of investment (outlined below) suited for your particular area.

If you're willing to drive a little bit, you likely have to ability to choose **different residential real estate investing strategies** because different locations are best suited for different investment types.

Once you build some confidence in your residential real estate investing abilities, you can form your **team of experts** (mortgage brokers, lawyers, real estate agents, home inspectors, handyman, and property managers) in far off cities and achieve success.

Let's break down what I look for when choosing an area:

1. I'm always looking for **transportation routes**. Existing ones like commuter train lines, highways, and bus and/or subway transit systems.

Even better than existing transportation routes are **new** transportation routes. New highways, especially. They bring more people, and more people increase the demand in an area and the economic activity.

A new highway will often be a **major leading indicator** that an area is going to go appreciate strongly.

If the area I'm doing any residential real estate investing in is **easily accessible** to people, it makes it more attractive. Sounds simple, but it's true and **often overlooked**.

2. **Demographic trends**. Is the population of the area increasing or decreasing? More people = More demand.

3. **Economic activity**. Is there an increase of jobs in the area? More businesses? More business parks planned? More jobs = more people.

If you look at any of the growing suburbs around Canadian cities, you'll see a **very common trend** that you can use to your advantage.

New highways will go into an area, and then the very first new residential subdivisions will follow.

The first new big box retailers will then **begin setting up shop**. And then, an influx of additional residential builders will build some more homes around these big box outlets.

Watching out for new highways is an easy way to spot areas that will appreciate well.

If the new highway is cutting through an established neighborhood, you will still see infill development projects by smaller builders and big box stores muscle their way in.

Population trends can be tracked at a provincial level from Statistics Canada. You can check out the Census Trends website for more information.

A quick search on Google for any city will turn up some great **detailed population**, immigration and employment trends that are key when determining if you are in an area that is appreciating or **will** appreciate shortly.

If you keep looking, it's easy enough to find immigration and population data and trends for the individual communities in your city/town.

A Little Tip for You...

You can easily **analyze demographic** data until your head swells.

There's another way to get similar information.

Use the information that we discussed above **to your advantage**.

When you see a bunch of new retail shopping stores being built in an area, this signals great **opportunities** for your residential real estate investing.

If you see a Home Depot, Wal-Mart, Cineplex, Loblaw's, Best Buy, Home Outfitters etc. being built, it's a great sign that the area **is appreciating** or will soon.

These companies have teams of people analyzing demographic data. **Why not** piggy back off their research for your residential real estate investing?

If they are plunking down big bucks to put up these retail properties, you can bet they have spent the time to analyze the decision.

Better yet, call up your city planner and get public information regarding the development of these stores even before the first shovel hits the dirt.

Knowing where the next Wal-Mart is going in **before the masses** puts you in a great negotiating position!

Perhaps the residential investment property you are putting an offer in on is about to be worth **much much more** than the seller's believe.

Doing a bit of **homework** can really make your returns jump nicely.

Most people will just blindly purchase properties based on some sort of tip or because they see everyone else lining up in front of a new condo sales office.

Look, when you see line ups outside condo developments with price increases every hour on the hour, you won't find experienced investors any where in sight.

They're the ones selling the condos at that time, not buying.

Always watch what the masses are doing and do the opposite...you'll be in **good shape**.

-- Residential Real Estate Investing --
Pick A Strategy

When you are residential real estate investing, you want to pick a strategy or investment type that works for the **specific part of town** you are looking to purchase within.

Will you choose regular single family home rentals, student rentals, and multi-unit dwellings? You should ask yourself these **two questions**...

Do you want to **Buy & Hold** real estate to create long term wealth?

OR

Do you want to **Buy & Flip** real estate to make immediate income? (Note: this strategy is less about investing and more about creating income for yourself.)

4
Financing Investment Properties Three Often Overlooked "Gotchas"

When financing investment properties, most investors make the **same mistakes**. This is important and it is the most common situation I see beginner real estate investors get themselves into.

You go out and get pre-approved by your **mortgage broker** for an investment property mortgage in Canada.

They give you the **thumbs up,** and tell you to go out and purchase your first investment property.

You are excited that you have begun your **wealth creation journey**. And you should be -- real estate is a proven vehicle to build wealth!

You then go and find a Real Estate Agent that **knows something about investing in real estate**, you spend weeks finding the perfect property and you finally make the purchase.

Then it happens...

Closing day approaches and your mortgage broker rings you up with something like this:

"Hey, I've got some updates. Apparently I can't actually get that mortgage program that we spoke of a few weeks ago. Don't worry, you will still be able to purchase the investment property, but you'll need to put down 10% instead of 5% and the interest rate on the mortgage is going to be 7.8% instead of 5.9%."

Now you've got problems. You need to magically come up with more cash, your **Return on Investment** will change drastically and your monthly **cash flow** on the property will go from a positive to a negative.

Let the scrambling begin!

You call your agent, who will likely **not have many options** for you. You call another broker, who doesn't have enough time before closing to **save you** and you then call your mom asking to borrow money to save this deal from falling apart. Not fun, not funny.

You Must Ask Questions to Get the Critical Financing Details
Here's what you should know about financing investment properties:

1. First off, always ask your friendly neighborhood mortgage broker how many investment properties they have actually closed on. **You are looking for experience.** Let someone else work in a beginner. Not you, it's not worth your time or your money.
2. Secondly, ask the mortgage broker to send you the **fine print**. Ask for the details of the mortgage program for financing investment properties.

Check that the interest rate on the mortgage program doesn't have any clauses about **increasing the interest rate** based on your down payment amount. I've seen brokers offer mortgage programs without fully understanding the program.

You should know that these mortgages for financing investment properties are **hyped and sold to the brokers** just like anything else: with salespeople and marketing flyers.

Some of the marketing material may highlight a certain interest rate. But the fine print may state that your credit score must be above 650 AND the down payment must be 15% to qualify, not 10% as you anticipated.

Now let me be clear. I don't think there's any malicious intent in these situations. There's fine print in every deal, whether it be a car purchase or a **commercial lease** or financing investment properties.

However, if your **banker or mortgage broker** hasn't been through any investment mortgages, they may be totally unaware of these critical points.

So take it upon yourself and ask them to **email or fax** you the details of the mortgage program.

3. Lastly, know your credit score. **You can pull your credit score** from Transunion or Equifax and it will not affect your score.

When you pull your credit score yourself it's called a '**soft pull**'. Your credit score plays an integral part in getting any mortgage and it's **amazing how many people** don't know their own score.

You may think you have **perfect credit**, but, you forgot to pay a $20 VISA card bill 6 months ago and your score drops from 660 to 610 and **you now no longer qualify**.

Real Estate Investing is a **real business**. Treat it as such. Know you broker's background, know the details of financing investment properties, know your credit score, and ask questions!

It will save you **last minute panic attacks** two days before closing.

You can focus on making money instead of spending more of your own.

5
"To Get Rich in Real Estate Investing Know the Difference between How the Pros and the Amateurs Behave"

Look, it's 100% possible to make some real wealth, even get rich in real estate investing. Whatever your definition of "get rich" may be, you can accomplish it with real estate.

There's opportunity to earn both monthly passive income and large chunks of cash months after closing on a property.

But, you need to know what you're doing and we constantly see beginners make mistakes. Mostly, because they don't follow the basics of getting some education, then finding a mentor and then following a system. .

One of the most important aspects of real estate investing is advertising and filling your property with a tenant. After all, having someone pay you money every month is kind of the idea. That's one of the important ingredients if you are going to get rich in real estate investing.

Here's something that we've noticed over the last couple of years.

Anyone can take a project to 90% completion. It takes a real pro to finish the job. And it's that same pro who gets to reap the rewards of a finished project.

Getting a tenant into a rental property is obviously worth a good sum of money to a real estate investor. Depending on the rental program used, there may be an immediate windfall on the line.

For example, if you are renting out a single family home using a lease option, the successful placement of a tenant is worth thousands of dollars to you on day one and possibly tens of thousands of dollars to you after a couple of years.

There are four important differences between an amateur real estate investor and a real professional. These four can mean the difference between selling a property at a loss to rid yourself of it and making very healthy returns.

Amazingly, you don't have to be a marketing genius to fill a property with a good tenant but you do need to do these things:

1. **Constant Presence.**

    Let's say you advertise your property for a week in the local paper. Towards the very end of the week, you line up a tenant for your property and set a date two days later to sign the lease and pick up some cash as a deposit to hold the property.

    You are excited and to save a couple of hundred dollars, you stop advertising in the classifieds for the next week.

    The meeting day rolls around and of course - it happens.

    One of you has a kid that is sick, or a dog that needs surgery, or a car that isn't behaving and you need to reschedule.

    Then, for no reason whatsoever, when you try to meet up on the agreed upon rescheduled day the possible tenant vanishes. Calls aren't returned, their voice mail box is full and their girlfriend, who you called because you were smart enough to get a back up contact number, has no idea who you are.

    Frustration settles in.

    You begin to wonder if you can ever get rich in real estate investing.

    You have no more tenant leads because you stopped your advertising. To save a few hundred bucks, you pulled your advertising and all the momentum you were building is lost.

    The other possible tenants have vanished and you need to start all over again.

You then resort to questioning human nature. A popular question asked at this time by beginners is "Why do these tenants lie? They said they wanted the house, why don't people do what they say they'll do? What's wrong with people these days?"

Nothing is wrong with people. People have behaved this way for hundreds of years and will continue to do so.

The problem is you, not them.

It's your lack of sales experience and knowledge that is the problem. You focus on the negative, and it's a downward spiral from there.

We've seen this happen to amateurs over and over.

It ends up being so scary at this point, some people just break down and decide that they can't get rich in real estate investing and leave the game all together. It's a bad idea, but to each their own.

Now, the professional does the opposite.

The professional investor keeps advertising until the lease is signed and there is cash in their pocket. And not just on free websites like Kijiji or craigslist . They'll actually spend the money to keep a well written classified ad in the papers and on that paper's website.

A signed lease can represent tens of thousands in revenue.

You get rich in real estate investing by getting things like leases actually signed.

Why would anyone jeopardize that to save a few hundred bucks on advertising?

Small thinking produces small results and by cutting off advertising before you have a signed lease agreement you are thinking small.

The professional investor learns about human nature and realizes that people may not follow-up on commitments. However, the pros don't focus on that. Instead, they focus on having three or more possible backup tenants in the wings.

They continue to show the property to other possible tenants until the lease is signed. They attempt to sign the lease on the very same day that someone shows interest.

If that person doesn't have the full deposit on hand, they accept whatever it is they have in their pocket. They know that when someone coughs up even a partial deposit, they are emotionally tied to the property.

They leverage their other possible tenants to create a competitive situation.

The professional understands that momentum is key and works hard to create and maintain it.

To get rich in real estate investing you must never stop advertising until everything is signed, sealed and delivered.

Never.

2. **A Good Yard Sign Right on the (surprise!) Front Lawn**.

Now, one may seem obvious, but we've seen amateurs screw this up.

It's amazing to me that someone will buy a property for a few hundred thousand dollars, and then invest zero or next to zero on a good yard sign.

Or buy one but let it sit in the trunk of their car (I can only assume there is a pool of possible tenants in their trunk and that's why it's there).

If you are going to get rich in real estate investing you must put in a yard sign.

We have found that a HUGE percentage of tenants for student rentals, regular single family home rentals and lease option rentals come from the immediate surrounding area.

It's either a friend walking by the house that sees the sign and passes on the information, or a family member who lives in the area and is looking for a place for their extended family or someone out on a drive just scouting the area for a good home.

And those little 8" by 9" black and red "For Rent" signs don't count.

You need a big professional sign --the type a realtor would use. You want this thing to stand right in the middle of the lawn using a solid frame to hold it up.

Home made signs fall down, blow over, deteriorate to mulch in the rain and just don't get the job done.

Invest is a solid sign. You're looking at approximately $100 to do so. If you really want to get rich in real estate investing, you won't let $100 stand in your way.

Without it, people would have to be mind-readers to figure out your house is available for rent or for sale. Possible I think, but not common.

I'll leave this point with a story.

We were working with one investor who really wanted to get rich in real estate investing.

He spent thousands of dollars on training courses before he began working with us. He then took time to find a property, he ran all the numbers, lined up financing, set up a partnership with a family member and bought the house.

He ran some ads in the paper, but didn't put up a yard sign. He didn't think it was necessary.

Well, after a few weeks of not placing anyone in his rental property, he got nervous.

After chatting with him and learning he hadn't done the obvious thing and let people in the area know their house was available, we yelled at him. Again and again.

Until he went and put up a yard sign.

The very same week, a couple signed up to lease the home.

And, they made a comment that went something like this: "We were on this street last week looking for a place and didn't ever realize this home was available."

Ouch.

The professional real estate investor knows that to get rich in real estate investing, you have to take this business seriously.

Advertising your property with a basic yard sign may sound simple, but it's a key ingredient that beginners often ignore.

3. **Massive Action - this is a biggie.**

So many people have been handed things to them their entire lives, that when something doesn't go according to plan, they completely break down.

They freeze.

Deer in the head lights syndrome.

Here's what I mean. If an amateur investor doesn't get their property rented out quickly, they will start blaming the people that came through the house.

They'll blame the possible tenants for not "seeing" the value in the home, or for not following up. Or, for not having enough money to put together first and last month's rent.

The amateur blames everyone but himself. You will never get rich in real estate investing like this.

If a professional investor doesn't get a home rented out within a reasonable time, he/she goes into action, MASSIVE ACTION.

They do not just do one thing to try and fix the situation.

For example, if their yard sign was small they don't just go get a bigger one. The pro will get rich in real estate investing because he or she go off and do 10 things all at once.

A new sign, flyers to the area, improving the street appeal, working on their sales skills, seeking advice from a mentor, changing their ad, introducing a voice mail system instead of answering calls live so they aren't fumbling the phone in the car trying to answer calls, putting up directional "For Rent" signs on street corners... the list goes on.

All too often, the amateur investor will do one thing and think they've done enough.

Nothing could be further from the truth.

When the going gets a bit tough, you need massive action to create momentum.

Massive action is what will allow you to get rich in real estate investing. Action, lots of it.

Beginners move so slowly at improving their strategy that I think they actually bore themselves into losing interest!

They had a dream to get rich in real estate investing and then let it fade.

They have no commitment.

It's nuts.

Move quickly, because it's really the only way to get things done.

That leads us to the final point...

4. **Taking Responsibility for the Results**.

    Professional investors ask questions about all situations. Then, they adjust their approach immediately.

    Amateurs point fingers. Professionals take responsibility.

    The amateur investor focuses on everything but themselves.

    The pro will always be asking themselves questions:

    Am I getting the proper number of leads from my advertising in the paper?

    Can I word my ads better?

    Is my yard sign visible?

    Can I improve the street appeal?

    What is the feedback from the tenants who have been through the house?

    Am I pushing people away with a hard pitch to rent out the home?

Are my price points set properly? Am I doing a good enough job explain the price and the value?

Where are people coming from to view the property? Can I advertise more in that area specifically?

They will take these answers and turn them into the massive action required to complete the job.

Remember, anyone can do anything up to 90%. It's the pro who takes it all the way.

To get rich in real estate investing you have to become a pro.

Will you?

6
What does Mountain Biking at Blue Mountain have to do with Real Estate Investing in Canada?

When you begin real estate investing in Canada it can be a really emotional ride.

Trying to figure out if the property you are about to buy will actually make you any profits can put you into a frenzy.

However, real estate investing in Canada is much like doing anything else for the first time.

A little while back my family took a trip up to Blue Mountain in Collingwood, Ontario. During the summer, they turn the ski hills into an amazing down hill mountain bike course.

I've never tried it before, but who am I to avoid something that looks like so much fun?

As I was waiting for my downhill lesson to begin, I couldn't help notice that I felt anxious and I was starting to doubt myself.

I didn't really know what to expect over the course of the next two hours.

The tough looking guy (ok, boy) next to me looked like he had 10 years of experience and he couldn't have been more than 17 years old.

I was sitting on a $5,000 downhill mountain bike on loan from the pro shop and for some reason, I almost felt like turning it in and running back to the safety of my hotel room.

Your emotions really play games with you when you try new things. No big surprise here, right?

Yet it amazes me that it's the exact same pattern we go through with all new experiences -- especially with real estate investing in Canada.

So, if we can recognize the pattern, we can learn to break through it!

It doesn't matter if you are about to ride down the side of a very steep hill or buy your first investment property. The steps are the same.

Here's my interpretation of what someone goes through during any new experience. I will use mountain biking and real estate investing in Canada as examples for each step:

1. You get excited about something (mountain biking or real estate investing in Canada)
2. Talk to people about it and get even more excited.

    Mountain Biking: "I'll be on the X Games soon"

    Real Estate Investing: "I'm going to be Donald Trump II"

3. Decide to get serious about it and track down some education.

    Mountain Biking: Visit the pro shop

    Real Estate Investing: Attend an education class or read a book on real estate investing in Canada

4. Learn the pros and cons. Analyze the worst case scenario.

    Mountain Biking: Some scrapes and bruises

    Real Estate Investing in Canada: The house catches fire, insurance rebuilds it and I sell the property. I then curse about real estate investing to all my friends.

5. Decide to take action!

    Mountain Biking: Rent a bike and take a lesson

    Real Estate Investing: Find a mentor and a property

6. HAVE THE FEAR OF GOD RUN THROUGH MY VEINS!

Mountain Biking: Tell myself that I can't do this

Real Estate Investing: Tell myself that I can't do this

>>> **DECISION POINT** <<<<

OPTION #1: Bail out at this point because the emotions get too difficult to handle.

Mountain Biking: I really shouldn't do this, why bother, I'm too old/hungry/slow/fat/thin/tall/short anyway.

Real Estate Investing: I really shouldn't do this, why bother, it's too scary/risky/unsafe/time consuming anyway.

OPTION #2: Stay committed; even after the initial excitement about the idea has faded.

Mountain Biking: "I'm going to beat this thing and love it, I CAN DO THIS!"

Real Estate Investing: "I'm going to beat this thing and love it, I CAN DO THIS!"

If you chose option #1:

Now that I have given up on this, I can start planning to give up (again) on my next decision. Never really doing or trying anything that feels uncomfortable.

Mountain Biking: "I'll come back and try this next year when I get a better night's sleep."

Real Estate Investing: "I'll try this next year when the moon is in perfect alignment with Mars and my credit line has 105 less dollars on it."

OR, if you went with OPTION #2...

Enjoy the rush of adrenaline, build confidence and realize that I CAN DO WHATEVER I WISH WHEN I STAY **COMMITTED**.

Mountain Biking: Feel the pride of accomplishment. Increase confidence for your next decision. Move on to bigger and even better things.

Real Estate Investing: Feel the pride of accomplishment. Increase confidence for your next decision. Move on to bigger and even better things.

I started to recognize this pattern happening to me when I was waiting for my mountain biking lesson to begin.

I chose to squash my fear based emotions and push on.

I didn't know what would happen during the next two hours on those hills, but as someone somewhere once said, "Those people who need to know everything before they begin really don't accomplish that much".

I agree. Strongly.

Whether it concerns mountain biking or real estate investing, go out and get some education, plan for the worst and then make your move!

You'll be glad you did.

Real life is the best teacher.

No book or course can replace actually doing something. And no book will make you rich without a strong COMMITMENT to taking ACTION!

I ended up flying over my handle bars after hitting a rock. That resulted in a few bangs and bruises but I pushed on and ended up having a blast.

And the best part, my son and niece now think I'm a super hero!

7
"When Buying Rental Properties, The Velocity of Money is Key!"

When buying rental properties, there are some key principles to follow.

Money responds to SPEED.

This applies to everything, not only buying rental properties. But for the purpose of staying on topic, let's focus on real estate.

When you move quickly with your decisions and your investments, money seems to find a way to move quickly into your pockets.

Sounds basic, but so many people don't get it.

After working with many investors, some beginners and some experienced, I've noticed a common theme emerge from them.

Let me illustrate with an example loosely based on a true story.

Let's take two investors who are looking at buying rental properties. Sally and Joe.

Sally is a beginner investor. She has never bought an investment before. She takes the time to get some education, finds a mentor and a system that is proven and then decides to act.

She buys a residential investment property, even though she feels that she really doesn't have all the answers to buying rental properties just yet.

But she's surrounded herself by a good team of mentors (experienced investors, attorneys, accountants etc.), so she makes her move.

Joe is looking at buying rental properties as well, and has started his search.

Joe learns that Sally has already made a purchase and lets her know that he would never move as fast as she did.

He finds a couple of great properties, does some analysis on the comparables in the area, drives around the neighborhood, and asks for family opinions and thinks of everything that could wrong.

Joe is also surrounded by a good experienced team with a proven system, but fails to leverage them.

Sally closes on her property and finds a few things that the home inspector missed and it kind of upsets her.

Rightly so, since you don't want your home inspector missing anything at all. But, she's now in the game. No turning back.

She makes a few calls to her experienced team and they tell her to move forward. She really has no choice. If she wants to succeed, she needs to get her place rented.

She puts up a sign, runs an ad and gets the property out there to rent it out. Within a few weeks, she has rented it out for higher than market rent and collected a down payment from the tenant.

Her new confidence propels her to purchase a second investment property weeks after closing on the first one.

During this time, Joe has still not purchased anything. He continues to analyze the potential problems and stays stuck.

Specifically, he read of a type of analysis where you take the property taxes of homes in the area and compare them to recent purchase prices.

The good homes he is looking at fall slightly outside of his desired ratios.

His experienced mentors advise him that the market is appreciating quickly in the area and is likely the cause of his ratios being off.

Based on their proven track record they suggest he move forward.

But Joe can't get his mind off of this property tax calculation and convinces himself that buying rental properties is not in his immediate future.

He fails to capitalize on the experience of his team and doesn't really even know the background of the calculation he is using. He just found it in a real estate investment book, written years ago by someone half way across the country.

So here we have two people with similar education, similar financial backgrounds, the same mentors and they end up with two different results.

I've seen this happen time and time again.

The people who are making money put themselves into money making situations.

They put themselves into the flow of money.

In the example we used, Sally was a novice but because she made a decision and then took some action, she was forced to make things work.

She hit a hiccup on closing but couldn't stay focused on it…there was not time for that.

She was facing the possibility of having to make a mortgage payment from her own pocket. She had to take action, she had to handle the pressure and get moving.

The looming mortgage forced her to have her property rented out by a certain time.

This organized her into taking a series of small actions (placing an ad, ordering a sign for the front lawn, calling people back, meeting them at the property) that ended up with a positive result.

It's only these types of real world deadlines and situations that get someone moving.

Read that again, it's important.

Now, I'm sure there is more than one of you saying to yourselves that in this example, Joe was doing his research. He was being a sophisticated investor who does his homework before making a purchase.

I agree. He was doing the right things by analyzing his purchase.

But I can tell you with 100% certainty...you do not make money by doing research.

You make money by taking action. Money responds to SPEED.

You need to do research and you need to surround yourself by a good team of mentors. But once have done that, you don't need to write a thesis on your decision before you act.

You'll never get anywhere. I've been stuck in that place myself.

I once found a property that was a "no brainer" but because I hesitated on making the offer, someone who made a decision locked it up for themselves.

When you put yourself in a place where you must act, the real world becomes your teacher, and that's the best education you can get. If you can handle it, the possibilities are endless.

The faster you take action, the faster money will find a way into your pocket.

So, do your homework, find some mentors and then take some action.

And by the way, in the actual true story of these two investors, Sally has continued buying rental properties and is on her third.

Joe dropped out sight. Probably got bored from the slowness (is that a word?) of his actions.

Too many people lose the chance to reach their dreams because they move so slowly that they literally forget why they are buying rental properties to begin with.

Money follows SPEED. Start moving.

8
Rental Property Investing With "Nice Homes in Nice Areas"

Here's something I'm asked all the time about rental property investing:

"Can you really make money investing in nice homes in nice areas? Everything I've been told says to buy run down homes in not so nice areas."

We literally had two construction contractors in our office a few months back, scratching their heads at the thought of making money from real estate without having to fix up properties.

Well, not only is it possible, it's my favorite strategy!

Before I explain why, let's look at buying run down properties a little closer.

From my experience, investors will buy properties that need some work for two reasons:

1. They want a "deal" that they can quickly sell for some profit.

   Now, I can understand the goal of making some quick cash from this, but is that really "investing"? Don't think so. Will this make you passive income that you can live off of one day? Ah, not really. Is this more like creating a job for yourself? Yup, it is. So although there is money in doing this, be aware of what it really is.

   You'll often hear people brag that they did a deal from their cell phone buying and selling run down properties without even seeing the thing. It sounds so exciting that people listening to that don't realize the person pulling that off has likely been in the real estate business for years and has a massive network of people finding these types of properties and another network of people interested in buying them. Don't buy the hype.

2. The second common reason someone will buy a run down property is to fix it up and then rent it out.

   Now, here's a strategy that I can live with. By fixing it up, the investor is creating equity in the property. If homes in the area are going for $200K and they bought this one for $160K, and then put in $20K worth of work into the home, they now have $20K in equity that they've created. I like it.

   And now they can rent out the property to create some cash flow.

I can truly respect this rental property investing approach. It's a great idea and will no doubt create a prosperous future for anyone who continues to do this.

However, is there a better way?

Is There a Better Way?

I think so...let me explain.

Investors typically use the strategy described in point #2 above because they can get a property for less than fair market value (because of it's condition).

As a result, their carrying costs may be lower and their cash flow position will be stronger when they rent it out.

Sounds good right?

But here's what most people forget. It will take you a few months to fix up the property and then rent it out, right?

Who is paying the carrying costs of the property during that time? You are.

Is your time worth money? It is, so what is that time you are spending on the property costing you? More than you think!

There's also some real, hard dollars spent to fix up the property. Who is spending that money? You are.

Who is dealing with the contractors used to fix up the property? You are. Or worse yet, who is working to fix up the property themselves? Ouch, hopefully not you.

Now, if you focus on rental property investing with nice homes in nice areas, there are some real benefits.

1. First, you can rent it out very quickly. Because it's a nice home, a family can move into it right after taking possession. This creates "incoming" cash flow instead of "outgoing" cash flow.

   Some investors actually rent out their homes even before they take possession!

2. Second, your property is in a nice area, so there are schools, parks, shopping malls, health care etc. all around you.

   These areas are in demand and typically appreciate well, so when the rising tide does hit the area, your home will be lifted with it.

3. And third, remember the time and money spent to fix up the property mentioned above? Well how about you take that and buy a second property? Now you have two properties working for you instead of one! Now you've leveraged your time and your money!

   In my opinion, that's much smarter.

And what happens to the person who is fixing up the property and then runs out of money? Can they rent out the property for top dollar? Not likely. Can they sell it and recoup their costs? Possible, but difficult.

Recently a client who used the "nice homes in nice areas" approach got talking with someone who bought a run down home to fix it up and rent it.

That person was driving for 90 minutes after work each night and on the weekends to fix up the property. From what I understand, they almost threw in the towel on rental property investing all together!

The toll on his life was just too much. He couldn't believe there were other rental property investing strategies he could have been using that would have saved him the months of driving back and forth. There are!

Can you imagine? He almost quit real estate investing. Before you let that happen to you, track down an investor working with nice homes in your area that you can learn from. It may save your investing career!

9
"Real Estate Investing for Beginners Means Keeping the Proper Perspective"

Real estate investing for beginners can be a confusing **maze of information and opinions** from family, neighbors, in-laws and the media.

One of the keys when beginning real estate investing is to keep the proper perspective.

Sometimes **you need to look at the big picture**, let me explain with a story.

So, there I was, about to be shoved out of a **40 year old plane** that was being held together with duct tape (I swear).

I was nervous, **sweating**, and praying that I would see my family again and just then, as I was looking around something hit me.

Right at that moment, I wished that **everyone** could be in this position!

Not because I wanted everyone to have the experience of possibly peeing in your **pants** as a grown adult, but because being so high up (2 miles above ground) gives you an **amazing perspective**.

Real estate investing for beginners can sometimes be a scary adventure, but after jumping out of a plane it can **get a lot less** risky looking!

We jumped out of a plane over Dundas, Ontario.

Dundas is **sandwiched** between Burlington and Ancaster in Hamilton, Ontario. It's a beautiful area.

And when you are heading up to altitude, you can clearly see the developments around the 407.

You can see the **traffic streaming** down the QEW and you can see the Hamilton Mountain traffic zipping along the LINC (Lincoln Alexander Parkway).

You also see the **widening** of Highway 6 off the 403.

It becomes completely obvious that the urban sprawl that started on the West side of Toronto is making its way right through this area.

And, when you have **huge investments** by the Province of Ontario in two major highway developments over the last 10 years (407 through Oakville/Milton/Burlington and the LINC finally connecting to the QEW this fall) and when Census Canada tells us 90,000 new immigrants a year land in the GTA, it is easy to draw **some conclusions**.

It's a great area for investors and especially for real estate investing for beginners.

More people in an area with increased transportation routes means more demand for real estate. Call me crazy, but I think it's obvious that **demand in this area** is going to increase over the next 10 years -- not decrease.

One of the major home builders already has a new subdivision butt right up against the 407 north of Dundas in Burlington. This area was **farm land** only a couple of years ago.

Oakville's town council has plans for the commercial industrial zoning and new residential **zoning** north of Dundas and south of the 407.

Mattamy's new sales offices aren't in Mississauga any longer, they are in Stoney Creek!

So when you are 10,000 feet above ground a few things become clear.

1. Real estate investing for beginners means **not** listening to the headlines in the paper that force the masses to think month to month. **Headlines** are created to sell papers, not to educate you.
2. **Think year to year, or better yet, decade to decade**. That's how proper investment decisions are made. The masses think month to month, so make sure you are thinking what will happen to an area over 10 year periods.

   Real estate investing for beginners is often not viewed with this perspective. Keep the big picture in mind. A mild **fluctuation** in interest rates should not shock you if you are looking at your investments in 10 year windows.

3. When you are that high up, the noise stops and you can clearly see what is happening. The clutter falls away.

So...

When about to invest in real estate, make sure you are looking at the **big picture**.

Don't get caught up in the hype around interest rates moving up or down 0.5% next month.

Think strategically, use the proper perspective.

Let the masses panic while you plow ahead and make the jump!

10
Forget Motivated Sellers, Find Nice Homes

Stop looking for motivated sellers, distressed sales, run down properties, or "the best deal".

Of course you can make money finding a sweet deal on an ugly house, but as a beginner at real estate investing, the time you invest to find that deal will be massive.

And, if you're not investing full time, you will be spending your nights and weekends away from your family, trying to fix up your 'super buy'. Is that what you had planned when you started? Have you turned yourself into a "real estate investor" or a "contractor"?

You have created a job for yourself. Add up all the hours you've spent finding the property, funding the property and then all the days you are at the property fixing it up. Then divide that by your anticipated profit. That's what you are paying yourself per hour. Sounds more like a job than investing to me. You're creating an income for yourself through some serious sweat.

I know many people making money like this. I have done it myself and will continue to do it.

But there is another way.

Why not find nice homes, in nice areas? Why not begin creating an asset base that works for you? Instead of selling the assets you buy, why not hold on to them? Isn't that what some of the best investors do? Buy assets and hold them?

Now, I'm sure we can turn this into a bigger debate, but think about it: isn't the point of getting into real estate investing to create some real wealth for yourself? The reason it's difficult to 'flip' properties is that there isn't a system for you to follow. When you're in the business full time, you'll have people call you up and deals will show up as your name becomes better known. But when you are squeezing this activity into your off hours, it can be challenging to find properties regularly. You may make a chunk of profit on one home and then you will spend the next six months driving around aimlessly looking for another deal.

Now do you think you are able to find nice homes in nice areas? A little bit easier right?

Nice homes attract nice people. Why not rent those homes out to them?

And what about cash flow?

Wouldn't it be nice to start generating some cash flow from your investment right away? Some positive cash flow, just as Robert Kiyosaki teaches in his Rich Dad Poor Dad books.

Well, it's all possible. There are specific strategies you can use to buy a nice home in a nice area, get thousands of dollars back from a tenant right up front *and* generate a positive monthly cash flow each month.

You will have tax deductions, equity build-up and appreciation. You can even set up your rental strategy so that there's a pot of profit after the rent term.

Doesn't this sound more like investing?

And it's possible to systemize every step of this strategy because there is a steady supply of nice homes and a good supply of people needing to rent.

So start looking at nice homes and extract cash flow from them.

Find a local investment club and start asking questions. These things are happening right in your own backyard.

Now go and do something!

11
The Real Estate Investing Basics of Single Family Rental Properties

Starting out, most of the real estate investing basics that I was **exposed** to around single family home investing was this:

"You, the investor, pays for the mortgage, insurance and property taxes. The tenant renting from you pays rent and utilities."

Even then I knew **there was more** to the real estate investing basics than that.

Let's cover some of it together. Good? Let's get at it.

When starting out, you want to pick an investment type that works for you and which moves you towards your real estate investing **goals**.

For example, single family home rental properties **will work best** in blue collar neighborhoods. By "work best", I mean that you'll get more people calling you for this type of property than if you do a single family home rental property in a higher end area.

And the investor who gets the most calls wins. Almost everything is a **marketing and numbers** game.

This is one of the key real estate investing basics that I found out well after I started buying the properties. It's worth repeating: *the investor who gets the most calls wins.*

Of course, you can still rent out properties in upper class neighborhoods. **I know people who successfully do it**. Just understand that you're appealing to a specific segment of the population, so the number of people that call your ads will be fewer.

So, as long as you're prepared to carry the property yourself -- **longer** than you would a smaller starter home -- you'll be fine.

The real estate investing basics around the returns you can expect to generate from your investment are as follows: regular single family home investment properties purchased in the right area can produce **cash flow, equity build-up (from the tenant paying down your mortgage), tax benefits and appreciation**.

ASIDE: Not many people discuss the real estate investing basics regarding appreciation so here it is. Appreciation can **never be guaranteed**. It is often discussed like appreciation is a sure thing. It's not. You can pick the most perfect area in the world but if a large "event" happens, appreciation may take much longer than anticipated. It may even go in **reverse** for a while. An event could be large and continuous interest rate hikes of the sort in the early 1990s, massive layoffs by a nearby employer, an oil crisis, national economic slowdown, etc. You need to keep a **long term perspective** (5-10 years) when residential real estate investing, and anticipate going through at least one major down cycle. If you know how your property will perform during the bad times, or at least plan for it, you'll be in good shape.

Depending on who you speak with, you'll get **different opinions on cash flow** and other real estate investing basics. Some real estate investing pros will tell you that positive cash flow properties are the only way to invest.

Others will tell you that appreciation will make you **more money** than a few hundred dollars in monthly cash flow. So, if the property is a negative cash flow property, it's well worth it, because you'll make thousands in appreciation.

There's a place for both but I would lean towards positive cash flow properties if I had the **choice**.

The last thing I want when investing in single family homes is a negative cash flow property that then goes on to lose value.

I'm then left with a property that I have to dump money into every month and may be **worth less** than the mortgage I have on it. Ouch.

I've had family members go through situations like this before, not fun.

Here's another one of the real estate investing basics. Each area and each property and each strategy has so many variables that you really want to sit down with someone and go over your strategy and investment types in detail.

It's **almost impossible** to give a blanket answer to cash flow questions without diving into the details.

Anyone that does probably doesn't have much experience or is trying to win an argument for **argument's sake**.

And there are ways to market homes to increase monthly cash flows and lock in higher than average appreciation.

That's the **beauty of residential real estate investing**. You are an active investor that can directly control your returns. And your options are almost limitless.

Plus, during your real estate investing career, you may purchase for **different reasons** at different times.

For example, would I buy a negative cash flow property knowing that a new subway line is being built that will bring thousands of people to my doorstep and will massively affect the property's value? **Yes.**

Would I buy a positive cash flow property in a not-so-nice area that appreciates slowly and there is no obvious pride of ownership? **No.**

These are my personal decisions and some of the real estate investing basics that fit my temperament and goals.

The best advice I can give you when picking a strategy and type of investment and implementing it is to find a **coach or mentor** that can teach you a system for investing in a particular area.

Getting current rental demand, rental prices, trends, infrastructure developments etc. is always easiest from someone actively investing (successfully) in the area.

"Rental Properties with a Twist"

Here's a little twist on some of the real estate investing basics.

You're probably pretty familiar with the idea of leasing a car and then having the ability to **buy that car** at the end of the lease.

You can do the same thing with rental properties.

You can lease the house to someone and **offer them the option to purchase it from you at the end of the lease.**

This does some wonderful things. The tenants get to move into a home that can ultimately become their own if they so choose. They get the pride of home ownership.

You will be able to ask for and get higher than typical rent from residential real estate investing like this. The property will, more often than not, be taken care of **very well** if the tenants are planning to own it.

Because of all this, you will have fewer management headaches with the property. **Fewer phone calls** about small issues (because they will take care of that leaky faucet themselves) and more peace of mind.

When done **properly,** this can work well for everyone involved.

This works best in areas where people are looking to settle down. Family-oriented communities, close to areas where people are renting are perfect. Your **typical starter home** is a property that you are looking for.

Every community has these areas. If you **don't** live in one, an area like this is likely within a 45 minute drive from you.

A question I often get is "Why we don't see more of this type of residential real estate investing in Canada?"

I can tell you from personal, **first hand experience** that these are happening all the time. There's just no national advertising campaign for it.

And there's just **no large builder** that is doing it regularly, so you don't see them advertised in the home sections of the local papers.

Most realtors haven't been exposed to any real estate investing basics, so **they don't offer them** as solutions.

And there's no "dealership" network for them, so it's left to the individual investor.

Henry Ford came up with the concept of car dealerships and this idea of his was responsible for getting automobiles into the hands of the masses.

These same dealerships are the ones that today offer cars on leases.

There's **no such network** setup to offer homes to people on these types of lease programs.

Basically, single family homes are too small for the big guys to get involved in.

Which is **great news** for your residential real estate investing career!

A word of caution, though: I've seen a lot of people **try and do these** the wrong way, use the wrong agreements, and charge the wrong amounts.

When using this strategy, make sure you are dealing with a real estate mentor and lawyer who have some experience with it.

So there you have it, the real estate investing basics on single family properties.

12
Learn About Real Estate Investing Using Student Rental Properties

When you are going to learn about real estate investing, you'll definitely want to hear the following debate.

You'll hear two drastically different sides when chatting about student rental properties.

There's one group of investors who absolutely love them. They are the **be all and end all** of their real estate portfolio and nothing can come close.

And then there's the group that has owned them and will **never touch one again**!

Hmm...Why such different opinions on this type of residential real estate investing?

Most student rental houses **cash flow extremely well**. Because you may have four, five, six or seven students sharing one house, your monthly rental income is nice and high.

Definitely a higher cash flow than if you rented out the house to a single family. I know one investor who has 9 students in one single family home...nine! (Done by the book, with permits, by the way).

His positive cash flow on this property is approximately $1,000/month.

So, with nice, high cash flows, some investors are attracted to these homes.

"Yeah, but what's the whole story?"

So what's the other side of the coin?

You've already guessed it, I'm sure.

Student rentals require **hands-on management**. Compared to regular, single family home rental properties, these have more maintenance issues and sometimes awkward vacancy challenges.

With five, six, seven, **even 9 students** in one house, there are going to be times when you have to deal with a broken window, door, light fixture, lock, tap etc.

Also, with so many people in one house, the **wear and tear** is pretty high on student rentals.

Another thing to keep in mind when you learn about real estate investing is how you will handle vacancies.

So, if one student can't stand another after a few months, they may **just pack up and leave** (I'm speaking from first hand experience here). If they break the lease and walk out, you're only real recourse is small claims court. And it's always the **smallest** bedroom that you are left with to try and rent out.

The rent on that one room may be the difference between having a positive cash flowing property and a negative one.

It can be difficult to find a student who wants to move into a house where they **don't know anyone**, right in the middle of a term.

You can get a good idea about the prices paid by students for housing by checking out the college or university housing website. They all have them. We used the one for the McMaster University in Hamilton, Ontario.

When you learn about real estate investing, ask around until you get some "on the streets" feedback from actual investors about their management experiences and systems.

I know people who have 20 single family homes and manage them by themselves on a part time basis. With 20 student rental properties, it will be a full time job for you or you'll have to use a property management company. Guaranteed.

Also, another thing to learn about real estate investing is that the mortgage programs can change at any time.

For example, financing student rental properties in Canada has become more **difficult**. You have to put much more as a down payment and some banks just flat our refuse to finance them.

Seems the Canadian banks and mortgage insurers don't want anything to do with houses that have a bunch of young adults drinking and partying in them at **all hours of the day**. They're busy making buckets of money elsewhere. They don't need the hassle.

Because of this, when you sell the property, you will be looking for a certain type of investor that wants that **specific** type of property and can navigate the financing waters to pull off the deal.

If you want to refinance the property, it can be more difficult because of what it is being used for.

So heads up! I wasn't aware that refinancing may be an issue until I actually tried to do one of my own.

The mortgage programs had changed from the time I purchased the property and there were a lot **fewer** options available.

Although the cash flow is nice and high on a student rental property, my preference is still single family homes.

Something to learn about real estate investing with single family homes is that when they are rented out as single family homes, they can be **much more flexible** to you from a resale and refinance perspective.

As discussed, the monthly cash flow will likely be less, but the appreciation, tax benefits, and equity build-up will be just as strong, if not stronger. Plus, a portfolio of single family rental homes makes for a very solid real estate investing foundation.

13
Real Estate Investing Strategy "Be an Active Investor, Not a Passive One"

When chatting about real estate investing strategies, I often hear, "But, I don't want to be a Landlord!"

Question for you: **Why not**?

What else can you buy using leverage (other people's money - namely, the bank's) and have the people who live in it pay for it? **And you get to keep the thing**. I mean, this is a beautiful real estate investing strategy!

It's my strong opinion that being an active investor is the best real estate investment strategy for generating wealth.

Wealth is built by controlling assets and controlling the cash flow yourself. Not owning a **small stake** in them. Remember that.

Warren Buffett, one of the most successful investors of all time, didn't get to where he is by having **small stakes** in his purchases. He is an active investor.

He may have other people running the show at a particular company, but he is active in that he **controls the companies** he purchases.

Why wouldn't you want to do the same? Are you **just talking about** building wealth? Or do you really want it?

If it's the latter, your real estate investing strategy should be to become an active investor.

When I hear people say that they don't want to be a landlord, I think they've been **assimilated into the consciousness of the masses** who don't want to think for themselves.

The myth that being a landlord is a negative thing keeps a lot of good people **out of the game** and leaves a lot of opportunity on the table for us investors.

This is great news for you and for me!

Basic property management or creative "self-regulating" tenant strategies can easily handle any of the "leaky faucet" horror stories that people have. And this should be a part of your real estate investing strategy.

Residential real estate investing is just **not that** scary.

If you **write down** on paper the very worst thing that could happen, you'd be surprised at what you find.

It's probably the house burning down, and you have insurance for that. If someone doesn't pay you, you evict them. If they damage your property, you evict them.

ASIDE: Everyone has a story about how it took someone they know six months to evict a tenant. Well, I challenge you to get the details. They likely didn't take any action. It just doesn't take that long! My money says they didn't treat their property as a business and bought into someone else's drama for way too long and gave them 4 or 5 second chances -- and that's the real reason it took so long to evict their tenant. Don't believe everything you hear.

Many people have all the real estate knowledge they need, they just **lack the guts** to get started and use excuses about "being a landlord" to talk themselves out of it.

Don't let your real estate investing strategy be one of the excuses that stop you from getting started.

Think of the wealthiest people you know, and ask yourself this: Do any of them own real estate? **Bet they do.**

Let me give you a **real world example** of why being a landlord is a great thing. This is based on real world real estate investing strategy occurring often in Ontario:

1. Buy a $220,000 house with 5% down = $11,000
2. Have a tenant move into the property before the first mortgage payment.
3. Receive $10,000 in the form of a down payment, plus first and last month's rent within 60 days for a total of $13,100.
4. Have the tenant handle minor repairs in the house.

In what other investment can you put down $11,000 and have $13,100 in your hands within 60 days? And that's not the best part. You've done all this, **you have over a 100% return on your money and YOU STILL OWN THE PROPERTY**! Please, read that last line again.

Real estate investing is just a **beautiful thing**.

There are closing costs that aren't represented above, but that's for good reason; there are strategies to handle those as well.

Now I need to throw in the regular disclaimers and state that this doesn't happen on every single property when residential real estate investing. **But it does happen, and often**.

But for arguments sake, **let's say** that you are a rookie and you "only" managed a 25% return in 60 days, wouldn't that still make you jump with joy? It should.

14
"Cash Flow is a Mystery for Canadian Real Estate Investing Beginners"

Cash flow has got to be one of the most highly **debated topics** of Canadian real estate investing beginners.

So many beginning real estate investors will decide whether or not a real estate investment is **good or bad** based on the answer to this single question:

"Will the property produce positive monthly cash flow? Give it to me straight Tom, yes or no."

"I want a nice simple answer."

"With residential property prices going up so high I'll have to drive 24 hours straight north into the frozen tundra to find a property that cash flows these days."

Huh?

Basing your entire decision on the answer to the positive cash flow question is a very limited way to look at an **investment**.

Sometimes, there just isn't a one-word simple answer for you when you're looking to create wealth.

There are **several things** Canadian real estate investing beginners need to consider.

Numero uno...

How much money are you putting down on the home?

Most Canadian real estate investing **beginners don't realize** that it's only been since about 2006 that you can buy an investment property with 10% or sometimes even 5% in Canada.

It wasn't that **long ago** that my local TD Branch was telling me that I had to put down 25% or even 35% down on an investment property.

So, the first thing you need to consider is that **there was a time** when investors were putting down much more on the property as a down payment.

This lowered their mortgage amount, and therefore lowered their carrying costs, and thus resulted in a higher frequency of securing properties that produced monthly positive cash flow.

Today, Canadian real estate investing beginners have the opportunity to buy investment property with 10% down or even 5% down (**even 0% down!**) using standard mortgage programs offered by Canadian banks (no funky hard money loans or vendor take backs - although these can be extremely useful and we'll discuss them in another chapter).

There are a few other things to consider.

Like, what are your **financial goals**?

Are you leveraging yourself for maximum advantage?

Are you using tax deductions like **you should**?

Are you **forgetting** that the mortgage is being paid down every month?

Let's take a look at this more closely...

Let's use a $250,000 property and assume that you have $55,000 to invest in real estate.

We could use a property of less value, but a **starter home** for $250,000 or less covers almost all regions across Canada.

For you Canadian real estate investing beginners in downtown Toronto or Vancouver, screaming that it's impossible, a 45 minute drive out of the city will get you properties like this.

A **25% down payment** on this property would look like this:

$250,000 Purchase Price
$52,500 required for 25% Down Payment
$1,055/month in carrying costs at 5.89% and a 40 year amortization
$225/month for Property Taxes
$55/month for Insurance
$1,335/month are your carrying costs

Can you rent out a $250,000 property in most parts of the country for $1,600/month or more?

Yes, definitely. Easily, even.

So, if you take the $1,600/month in rent and subtract the $1,335/month in carrying costs, you're **left with** $265/month in cash flow, right?

Well that's how most Canadian real estate investing beginners look at things.

But it's not uncommon to have at **least one or two** $300 expenses of some sort on the property throughout the year.

A **pipe leaks**, an electrical outlet stop working, a shingle goes flying off the roof, the furnace needs service...you get the idea.

When these hit on any given month, is **your property** still a positive cash flow property?

Hmm...yes or no?

Well most Canadian real estate investing beginners use a very **short window of analysis**.

Typically, they look at a **single** month at a time and then, when they get hit with that $300 repair, they'll scream something like this:

"My property isn't a positive cash flow property **any more**, the sky is falling!"

But they are focusing on too small of a window.

If they look at the **entire year,** they'll see that even with a couple of expenses, the property is still producing positive cash flow.

And here's where things differ between **beginner** real estate investors and experienced ones.

Experienced investors will look at the whole picture -- a 12-month period, **at least.**

They want their money to be working as hard a possible for them.

So, they **take into account** things like tax deductions, depreciation and appreciation before making any decisions on whether a property is a good investment **or not.**

Even if the entire positive cash flow every month is eaten up, they won't consider the property a loser.

The cash flow may be zero, but the **'tax flow'** may work to their advantage (Tax Flow is a term I picked up from one of our clients, love it).

Here's what I mean...

Canadian real estate investing beginners often aren't aware of all the tax deductions available to them.

By using these **deductions** (insurance fees, legal fees, property taxes, land transfer fees, maintenance, etc.) a property you thought was breaking even very well may be earning its keep.

Why?

Because tax deductions can often be written off against your other income and produce refunds for you.

The **depreciation** of the property should be able to do the same for you.

ASIDE: I'm amazed at how many Canadian real estate investing beginners don't use a professional accountant to do their taxes. A real estate accountant can really work magic with your tax returns. For the $250 it costs to use them, they'll save you at least double that in things that you didn't know how do deduct yourself. The wealthy use professionals, so should you.

From my experience, the middle class will focus on **short time frames** for analysis and to make decisions.

The wealthy look at the big picture and use a longer time frame.

They'll look at investments in ten year periods, **at least**.

The middle class will look at investments on a monthly basis and panic every month.

Canadian real estate investing beginners do the same.

Don't let that be you.

Look at the big picture.

Did you buy the property for a few hundred dollars in cash flow each month, or for the long term wealth that paying this property off will bring?

One More Thing Often Discounted By Beginners

Another thing Canadian real estate investing beginners completely ignore is that **equity** that is being built up in the property each month.

Every month that mortgage is being paid, you are earning a few hundred dollars in equity as the mortgage is paid down.

I know you can't **touch and feel** that, but wealth can be built consistently with this approach.

And what about appreciation?

You can never bank on appreciation, especially when using a window of 5 years of less.

Anyone that guarantees appreciation needs to have their head checked.

But over long **periods of time,** this is the most powerful accelerator of your wealth creation.

If your property appreciates at a rate of **5% over 5 years,** you're looking at healthy returns.

Let's use the example above.

The $250,000 property after year **one** is worth: $262,500

After year **two** it's worth: $275,625

After year **three** it's worth: $289,406

After year **four** it's worth: $303,877

After year **five** it's worth: **$319,070**

That's $69,070 in appreciation or 131% return on your $52,500 down payment.

Not bad.

And that doesn't take into account tax deductions or the equity being built into the property.

"But I don't have $52,500 to use as a down payment!"

Well, that's good news.

Yup, **great news**.

Let's say you have $20,000 to use...

We can use a 5% Down Payment for the property:

$250,000 Purchase Price
$12,500 required for the 5% Down Payment
$1393/month in carrying costs using a 5.89% 35 year amortization period and 4% for Mortgage Insurance (required in Canada b/c the down payment is less than 20%)
$225/month for Property Taxes
$55/month for Insurance
$1,673/month are your total carrying costs

Now let's assume you rented this out for $1,600 just as we did in the **previous example**.

You're negative $73/month.

But remember, we're smarter and wiser now, so we look at the property on at least a one year window.

So that negative $73 becomes $876 over the year.

Your tax deductions alone should make you that back in tax deductions that result in refunds for you.

But let's not bank on that.

Let's say you had to use a portion of the $20,000 you had to invest to cover that $876 every year for five years.

Earlier we agreed that at 5% appreciation the property is worth $319,070 after five years.

That's $69,070 in appreciation or an amazing **553% return** on your down payment of $12,500.

And if you had the original 25% to put down on the property, wouldn't it make sense to **buy two properties** instead of one?

Now you are leveraging your money and the few hundred dollars in positive cash flow you are passing on to do it becomes **chump change** in exchange for the leverage you create for yourself.

Don't get caught in the Canadian real estate investing beginner trap of **just focusing** on the monthly returns as the basis for your decision making.

Now let me be clear.

I'm not telling you to jump on any property because it's OK if it's not producing positive cash flow.

That's wrong.

You still need to **do your homework**. You should still be working with a **mentor**, and you should still be picking a **good investment**.

In other articles, I explain why and describe the scenarios in which I would jump on a negative cash flow property.

The **purpose of this discussion** is to expand your thinking a little. To get you thinking like experienced investors think.

Can We Maximize This Even More?

Now that we've discussed that a negative cash flow property may not be such a bad thing if managed correctly...**let me throw you a curve ball.**

Wouldn't it be great if you could make the property you put 5% down on **produce positive cash flow**?

And wouldn't it be great if you didn't have to **pay closing costs** out of your pocket so that you could save that money to buy more properties?

15
"The Top 10 Mistakes Made On a Canadian Real Estate Investment"

You can't get involved with a Canadian real estate investment and not expect to **at least make one** mistake.

But here's the thing, I never look at mistakes as a bad thing.

We always ask beginner investors to make as many mistakes as fast as possible. It's the only **way to learn**.

Let me put include a little **caveat** here...the beginner investors we work with are working with our team, following a system, and we're assisting in the **selection** of the Canadian real estate investment and advising on different strategies to use with the property.

So **we know** they've chosen a good property and we know the strategy they'll be using to make money on the property because **we are implementing** it constantly.

So, when we ask beginners to make mistakes, we're usually referring to the process of filling their property with a tenant.

You don't want to make too many mistakes when choosing your Canadian real estate investment or the **strategy you use** to profit with it. Mistakes there can have rather serious financial impacts on you, and quickly!

Most people are scared to make mistakes when showing their property to tenants or afraid that they'll **say the wrong thing** when talking to possible tenants. Or they're afraid they'll pick the wrong tenants.

You should know that everyone feels this way.

It's 100% normal.

Don't freeze up. It's during this process that you should just go off and make as many mistakes as **quickly as possible**.

Here's why...

The **more quickly** you make the mistakes and screw up talking to possible tenants, the more quickly you learn.

If you turn a tenant off because you present the property incorrectly or don't position the rent you are asking for **with confidence**, or if you don't create the property environment to rent out your property...big deal!

You've just learned **what not to do**.

Getting someone else to look at your Canadian real estate investment **is not difficult**. And now, because you've made some mistakes, you're better prepared for the next person you speak with.

Many beginners are so scared that they'll say the wrong thing when trying to rent out their Canadian real estate investment that they'll spend time on non-revenue producing activities.

This includes fixing things that **don't need fixing**. Such as calling for quotes on a roof repair that still has 5 years life on it. Or, spend time running the numbers on their property for the 110th time.

To make money on a property, you need to focus on the few activities that make you money. **Read that again.**

Fixing a door knob isn't one of them.

You need to get someone into your property so that you can collect cash.

With all that said, let's **jump** into the top ten mistakes we see with investors and their Canadian real estate investment:

"And the Top 10 Mistakes Are..."

1. Taking way too long to place ads for your property after it closes. Not creating momentum. Taking too long to call leads from your ads back. Calling leads one time and never calling them again!

2. Focusing solely on the monthly cash flow only, instead of the big picture. That includes: equity build-up, tax benefits, and possible appreciation.

3. Getting scared off during a home inspection instead of working to negotiate a solution that works to your advantage.

4. Making individual appointments with prospects instead of creating a competitive environment.

5. Working with a mortgage broker who has no idea how to handle investment properties. Working with a lawyer who has no idea about investment properties, or working with an accountant who has no idea about investment properties!

6. Not having an experienced mentor to help you. A good mentor can save you a great deal of time, money and help you avoid mistakes.

7. Not treating investing as a business.

8. Not following a step-by-step system. Too many investors "wing it."

9. Trying to find a deal vs. studying market demand. A good deal means nothing if there isn't any demand for the property.

10. And my personal favorite...trying to save a $100 negotiating a purchase and losing $30,000 in future profits!!

And there's something to **note about this list**. This is the general top 10 mistakes list.

There's a top 10 list for each step along the process and for each type of investment!

We'll get to **all of them** sooner or later.

Here's a quote that summarizes our thinking on making mistakes:

> **"If you don't make mistakes, you're not working on hard enough problems. And that's a big mistake."**
> - Frank Wilcezek, 2004 Nobel Prize Winner in Physics

Now go out and makes some!

16
Canadian Real Estate Investments: Real Stories from "The Streets"

Whenever you look for Canadian real estate investments, you end up researching online. I find a lot of real estate articles that focus on the "Top 10 Mistakes" or the "Most Important Numbers You Should Know" or "Accounting Essentials".

Basically, there's a lot of theory on Canadian real estate investments, and I'm guilty of writing these things myself.

But when you're starting out, sometimes real stories from real investors give you the most insight.

And it's because most people spinning out these real estate investing articles don't actually work directly with any investors that there's a gap in the information they provide. I'm not 100% certain they even work with any Canadian real estate investments at all.

I think that feeling comes from the first person that was going to sell me some Canadian real estate investments. His advice was this, "Buy them, real estate appreciates". And because I didn't know any better at the time, I missed out on asking a ton of other stuff.

Let's park the theory part and get to the real stories of real investors in the real world working with real Canadian real estate investments.

The kind of stories that come from working "in the trenches" and being "on the streets" and getting things done.

Ready? Let's go...

The Case of "I Want To Sell It!"

We were working with one investor who purchased a great single-family home investment property just outside the Greater Toronto Area, and wanted to sell the darn thing just two weeks after buying it!

I think her words were something like this: "I'm done with all Canadian real estate investments. I don't think this is for me!"

Ouch!

If she tried to sell it at that moment, she would likely have lost at least $15,000 because of the commissions and closing costs involved. That's no laughing matter.

When the real emotions of fear and anxiety kick in, all those great books that teach real estate investing (think Rich Dad, Poor Dad or Millionaire Next Door) get thrown out with the trash.

Emotions are powerful things, and you need to fight to keep logic from escaping you when this happens.

This investor closed on the house and then didn't do very much of anything to get a tenant to rent out the place.

Buying any Canadian real estate investments is only part of the process. You need to keep going and get your property rented if you're going to profit from the thing.

She actually did place one classified ad for one day, but that's it.

Well, I can tell you from direct experience that one classified ad for one day is better than nothing, but it's not enough.

The crazy part is that off that single little ad, she had a call from someone interested in the home, but she turned them down because they didn't "sound" like a good fit. The decision wasn't based on any facts.

The fear of having a mortgage payment approaching and not having a tenant in the house was apparently too much to bear and she started acting irrationally.

So we stepped in and settled her down. We asked her to focus on the little things.

Forget the big picture for a moment. Forget building your empire. Forget buying 15 other Canadian real estate investments. Forget equity build-up, possible appreciation, tax deductions, cash flow, forget it all.

We just asked her to focus on one baby step at a time.

Place an ad for your house. Answer the calls. Get people to the house. Get applications. Accept a tenant.

That's it.

Don't focus on the mortgage payment. Don't focus on any "what if" scenarios that are likely not going to happen.

Don't go and shovel the driveway 7 times a week (shoveling doesn't make you money - getting a tenant into the house does).

And as soon as she focused on the little important activities, things began to flow.

Calls came in from her ad. She met people at the property.

And you know what? Within one week of "re-focusing" on the activities that make money, she got a tenant.

She even managed to collect a few thousand dollars right up front.

Job well done. Disaster averted.

The Case of "The Shiny Object"

WARNING: What you are about to read is not PG rated. Stop here if you only watch G rated Disney flicks.

Have you ever seen a chicken running around with its head cut off?

A foreman that used to work for my dad's drywall company used to say he was working like a chicken with its head cut off.

I never really understood it until I visited my Aunt in Europe and she actually cut off the head of a chicken and let the body of this thing take off running in all sorts of directions.

Kind of like real estate investors running from one networking group to the next.

OK, the not-so-appropriate analogy is over.

But it serves a point.

So many investors get caught up in the hype of the next "big idea".

We worked with one investor recently who was distracted by every new investing idea (or "shiny object").

"I should invest in Alberta!" And then he would go off and research Alberta for a few weeks.

"I want to buy 15 Canadian real estate investments next week in BC with all the money from Asia landing on its shores!"

"I should invest north of Toronto in cottage country" And then he would go off and spend time looking at cottages.

"I should invest in the U.S.!" And then he would go off looking for a lawyer to setup up Nevada corporations for investments that they haven't made yet.

"I should buy a house and flip it or assign a contract for quick-easy-cash!" And then he would go off and network with other investors who are all trying to assign contracts to each other.

"I should invest in condo conversions!" And then he would run around looking for condo conversions in Cambridge, Ontario.

After a few months of this, he still hadn't made a single purchase of anything.

Zero Canadian real estate investments to his name.

In the meantime, another investor that started investing at the same time as him had purchased three nice single-family homes and had them rented out. And because he was actively investing, other opportunities just started popping up. For his third home, someone had found him and asked him to buy them a property that they could then rent from him.

They picked out the property and gave him first and last month's rent up front to show they were serious, so he then went out and purchased the property for them and had them move in on the day of closing. No advertising, no lag between closing and the time someone moved in. Pretty neat stuff eh?

Because that investor was not distracted by every shiny object that popped up, he was able to start creating his asset base that will create long term wealth.

Shiny objects are great and we're all guilty (myself included) of being drawn to them.

But the way to get ahead is to pick a course of action and stick with it.

You buy one investment property, then another, then another and before you know it, you have a stable of Canadian real estate investments working for you.

You can make money right in your own backyard using proven real estate strategies.

Don't get distracted by shiny objects and you won't fall victim to the "chicken with its head cut off" investing strategy. It doesn't work very well.

The Case of "I Want What I Want!"

One investor recently got so caught up in how much his monthly carrying costs would be on a property, that he wasn't willing to negotiate anything.

He ignored all the other benefits he would be receiving as part of his Canadian real estate investments and just focused on one thing.

He wanted to get $1,700/month in rent.

Period.

No negotiation.

He had a couple of great tenants come through the home and he sticker-shocked them with the price. Other homes in the area were renting out for $1,500.

Then he had someone offer him $1,600 a month and they could move in the very next month.

He turned them down!

He then finally got someone to agree to $1,700, but they needed to give 60 days notice at the beginning of the next month, so they couldn't move in for about 10 weeks.

And now enough time had passed that he was started to get desperate, so he accepted them.

If he hadn't been so firm in what he was looking for, he could have accepted the people for $1,600/month and had them paying him within a couple of weeks.

He would have been down $100/month, but over 12 months he would have actually been ahead, because the house wouldn't have been sitting vacant for three months!

Find common ground with your tenants.

Your Canadian real estate investments should be treated as a business.

And business requires constant negotiation. Get used to it.

The Case of "Advertising Is Too Expensive"

Recently, an investor working on her Lease/Option investment property was growing concerned about how much she had to spend to advertise her property.

ASIDE: A lease/option is when you lease out a house and the tenant who moves in also has the option to buy the house from you at some point in the future. Kind of like leasing a car.

It was going to cost about $245 to run a classified ad in the paper for a week.

She didn't lock anyone up for the property after that first week, and resorted to free classified ads online to "save" money.

Now, in our past experiences with Lease/Options, clients have been getting $5,000 or higher as an option payment, plus rent money. Several have received $10,000, plus first and last month's rent.

If you have to spend $500 or even $1,000 to get back $5,000, it's not a bad investment.

So she wasn't looking at advertising as an investment, she was looking at it as an expense.

Dangerous mistake (one that's made in most business, by the way).

With a little push, she started advertising again and got $4,000 up front, plus first month's rent.

That's a lot better than a vacant house!

Advertising is an expense to the tax man, but it's clearly an investment to you and your business of real estate investing.

Remember, the key to getting what you want is almost always looking around and doing the opposite of what everyone else is doing -- especially with your Canadian real estate investments.

She looked around and saw everyone advertising with free classified ads. So she did the same.

Never follow the crowd.

When you're starting out, you don't see the big picture.

It can feel like you're putting pieces of a puzzle together in the dark.

Stick with it...when you commit to getting it done, things fall into place - every time.

And with proper patience, your Canadian real estate investments (when bought properly) will become a foundation of your wealth.

17
Canadian Real Estate Trends are More Important than "The Numbers"

Sometimes it's more important to look at the Canadian real estate trends instead of just focusing on "**the numbers**" of an investment property.

Let me explain in a kind of roundabout way...

There's a pretty commonly held **belief system** amongst most of the people around me who have achieved their goals.

It has even **occasionally** been discussed "out in the open" - but it's rarely followed by the masses.

And for most people who don't want anything more than being "comfortable" with their lives, it's often ignored.

Ready for it? Alright then, here we go...

Instead of me wasting thousands of keystrokes trying to explain it, let me use a quote from **Earl Nightingale** that sums up what I'm referring to perfectly:

"If no given model for success exists in your chosen field of endeavor, then just do the opposite to the masses, and you'll win every time"

Read that one more time, and **read it slowly, let it sink in**.

From being exposed to the **construction industry**, software, **sales**, engineering, **farming**, raising kids (still in process) and **real estate investing,** I'm willing to go out on a limb and conclude that from my experiences, this statement is universally applicable to everything.

Yes, **everything**.

If you just look around and watch what the majority of your friends and neighbors are doing -- and then do the opposite -- you'll likely end up closer to your goals.

Even professionals, who should know better, get infected with a "herd mentality".

I'll give ya an example:

Years ago, I was reading every book, **every article**, every email, every thing on real estate investing and Canadian real estate trends that I could get my paws on.

My **journey,** ultimately, lead me to a mortgage broker who handled an amazing amount of investment property financing.

As I was picking her brain in **her office,** she said something to me that I took as law.

She was the expert right?

"Tom, I don't need to see the property, just show me the numbers. If the cap rate is right, then you should make a deal. That's how all real investors work".

Really?

For a few **years** afterwards, I kinda lived by that philosophy.

If the income minus the expenses **looked good, then it was a good deal, end of story**. I basically ignored all the larger Canadian real estate trends that surrounded the property.

I even repeated that to others. "Just show me the numbers, if the numbers look good, let's make an offer".

I was **analyzing small apartment buildings** and looking at the cap rates. Nothing looked too good in the Greater Toronto Area, so I began looking out of the big city.

I even had the mortgage broker start **emailing** me properties that were for sale with "good cap rates".

Well, the properties with decent cap rates were hours out of the city and they were in nasty condition. Really nasty.

And it finally hit me! These things have **good returns** because they're cheap. And they're cheap because they're dumps.

And these dumps were in the **middle of no where**!

So although the numbers looked good, these properties had **vacancies** that had to be dealt with, the location was not in a desired market and for my name to be on the property, I was going to have to invest in badly needed improvements.

This idea of "just show me the numbers" is flawed...
I no longer cared that "all real investors do it".

Remember: do the opposite of the masses.

There's more to investing than the numbers on the property.

You need to focus on the Canadian real estate trends that surround your investment. And then look at the numbers within the context of those trends.

Ultimately, the big Canadian real estate trends in rates, transportation, employment, neighborhood redevelopments, and zoning can have huge impacts on your investment.

And then "the numbers" on your one specific property don't matter much. A big trend can turn them upside down and spit them out.

On top of the big Canadian real estate trends, there are neighborhood trends, street trends and building trends.

There's a whole boat load of questions to ask yourself:

Is the property a winner?

How will financing work?

Is there demand for it?

Can you increase rents because of poor management and poor marketing?

What is the town planning department up to?

Any businesses moving in/moving out?

Are improvements necessary within five years?

I forgot all about this whole way of thinking until over the weekend, a beginner real estate investor told me they had made an offer on a triplex because the cap rate was good.

Upon further interrogation, I found that the wiring of the building would have to be replaced for a cost of $8,000-$12,000.

So they were about to buy this **property** because "the numbers looked good", but were immediately going to put in $8,000+ of their own cash to bring the wiring up to snuff.

They **didn't seem able** to connect the dots. The cap rate was good because the property needed work.

And they were ignoring any Canadian real estate trends all together.

They were so **blinded** by the cap rate on the building that they were overlooking the big picture.

They were going to have to spend over **$10,000** on it within months of taking ownership.

Just like everyone else. Well, not quite everyone ;)

The more **I think about it**, the more I realize that I constantly see people investing into properties with this way of thinking – while completely ignoring Canadian real estate trends.

Not the **best way** to do things.

So how would I look at the property? I would want to look at the numbers within the context of the **bigger picture**:

1. What are the major Canadian real estate trends in interest rates and demographics? Population increasing or decreasing? Any new transportation routes?
2. How is employment in the city? Any upcoming changes?
3. What part of the city is your investment property in? A growing area or a declining area? Even growing cities have areas you don't want to be in.
4. Any trends to the types of buildings in the neighborhood? Are a lot of rental properties popping up, a lot of tear-downs?
5. To remain competitive with other properties in the area, will there be a need for any renovations over the next three to five years?
6. Buy and hold? What is the exit strategy?

The next time a **bunch of investors** tell you to just look at the numbers, make sure you don't forget about the big picture.

You don't want to do what everyone else does.

And if you have been following the **herd**, now is the time to break from it.

Oh yeah, **I forgot to mention**. I've made this exact same mistake myself.

If I hadn't spent $20,000 a few years after purchasing a property to **renovate** the kitchen and bath, I could have bought another property!

Too bad at the time "the numbers" **looked good** and I was following the herd.

Focus on the long term Canadian real estate trends, and use them to pick investments that will benefit from them.

18
Knowing Your Credit Score Is Critical When Real Estate Investing

Your credit score is yet another topic that will greatly impact the quality of our life for its entirety, yet it is something we are never taught in school. (This seems to be an all too common trend)

Do you know your credit score?

If so, I applaud you, as most of us don't and probably never will until it is too late. When I refer to 'your credit score' I mean the FICO score that makes up a large portion of a credit report, so lenders can decide how much risk you pose and if they should lend you money.

To give you an idea of how this number is generated, the credit bureaus (Equifax and TransUnion are the most common) take into account these 5 things:

Payment history

Types of credit

Length of credit history

New credit

Current amount in debt

They use a formula that creates a number, and this number is tied to you for life. It can fluctuate, and the higher the number, the better your credit score.

Which class in school covered this? Or better yet, how often have you heard people speak of this? We are trained not to.

Yes, it can be a private matter, but in our society it is kept so private that most people have no idea what their score is and the importance of it.

As an investor and business owner, you should know what your credit score is, as it can drastically change your options when investing. Many of the most aggressive mortgage programs may only be available to people with great credit.

So, knowing and monitoring your credit can change the way you conduct business and can affect your profit and expense numbers, as well. It can be the difference between reaching your goals this year and taking two or more years to get where you want to be.

If your credit score is low you may not qualify for financing at all or have to pay a much higher interest rate with all sorts of lender fees.

If your credit score is damaged by missed payments, bankruptcies, etc., it can be fixed. Life happens, and sometimes it can take its toll, but it is important to find out what needs to be done to fix your credit score and get it back up.

Sometimes simply paying off one credit card completely -- even if it is only a small amount outstanding -- will immediately have a positive impact on your score. Make sure you realize that things can be fixed and if you end up with a bad score, take the necessary steps to correct it.

It may take time, but if you don't start now, when will you?

Personally, I always want mine to be above 700. My understanding is that if it is above 680 in Canada, you have a much easier time getting approved for many types of financing.

I like to keep it higher just in case there is a hiccup, it should not effect what I can do in my investing business.

OK, enough about the score. I think you get the idea. How do you find and monitor yours, you ask?

You can pull your credit score for free and have it mailed to you, or view it online for a small fee and get it instantly. Some people think any inquiry on your credit will affect your score, but it won't.

When you pull your own credit, it is called a 'soft pull' and does not have any adverse impact. You can find out yours at www.transunion.ca or www.equifax.ca

It can almost be scary when you see the records that are kept of you. But it is also empowering when you know what people will be looking at when you're building your real estate business.

To help your business thrive, know your score and if needed, do what it takes to get it up to where you want it. It will impact your options and profit moving forward. It will also help you talk to your prospects with a new found level of knowledge and confidence.

19
Canadian Real Estate Investing Experts: The 3 Types That Can Make or Break You

With Canadian real estate investing experts, there is a big difference between knowledge and implementation.

A huge difference.

There are so many different sources of real estate investing information, and so many Canadian real estate investing experts that you can get lost in information overload.

A quick search on Google will turn up books, audio programs, seminars, weekend boot camps and teleseminars -- all promising to be the best single source of information.

I've invested thousands (ok, tens of thousands - but don't tell anyone) into this type of stuff before I finally learned an important lesson.

The Canadian real estate investing experts that were dishing real estate investing ideas all had at least one little gem in their program, book or package.

But something important was missing.

There was no detail on how to implement a specific strategy in my own backyard. You are left on your own to figure that out. Perhaps that's why you know so few people actually real estate invest full time.

I tried taking "massive action". I called my local realtors, mortgage brokers, bankers, municipal power of sale departments and got lost, rejected or shut down.

It took years to realize that although these experts were teaching me sound investing principles, it was of absolutely no use to me out in the real world.

I needed someone who could show me the ropes. I needed a mentor, a guide, a coach. Just like a professional athlete. I needed someone to guide me, push me. Someone who had done it before me.

So I went off and built my team. A lawyer who understands creative real estate investing, a mortgage broker who knows how to maximize my investing power, an accountant who can structure my investments, a broker who is flexible with my requests. This was my very own swat team of Canadian real estate investing experts.

It took some serious time and effort, but benefits are huge.

And now that I have been doing this for some time, people ask me my opinion on a certain real estate investing program or package.

The answers are never the same, everyone has a unique situation.

But I can break Canadian real estate investing experts down into a few categories:

1. The "Eye Opener". I have the utmost respect for this category of expert. Robert Kiyosaki falls into this group and even though he is American, all Canadians can benefit from his information.

His *Rich Dad, Poor Dad* book offers very few specifics, but does an excellent job at explaining how real estate can change your life.

Kiyosaki takes a lot of unnecessary criticism, because he doesn't lay out detailed plans of action. But what his critics fail to realize is that his information opens your eyes to possibilities that you weren't aware of. That alone is the purpose of his work and it's done brilliantly.

Another "Eye Opener" would be someone like an aunt or uncle who has been investing for years. As a kid, you had no idea how they were able to get you the coolest birthday presents until one day you learn that they are active investors who use real estate to create wealth. And you have a big "ah-ha" moment in your life.

2. The next category is the "Traditional Expert" who sells boot camps, books and seminars. Now, let me start by saying that anytime I have invested in a real estate training workshop held by the Canadian real estate investing expert of the day, I always learn at least one thing, or meet one person that makes the entire event pay for itself. I'm a huge believer in constant and never ending education.

What I didn't realize, initially, is that sometimes these experts need to generalize their information to appeal to large audiences, so the information they give often needs tweaking to work in your specific market.

For example, when I learned about lease optioning, I was told that it couldn't work in my city because prices were too high. Then, another expert would tell me that lease options are completely underutilized in any market, no matter the price.

So the information I would get from these Canadian real estate investing experts was good, but the implementation of the idea was left up to me. I could ask them a few questions, even get them to spend a few hours with me, but I was on my own to actually make it work.

They were excellent at delivering the information, but really offered nothing more. Often, they were not even active investors in my own market.

When you are investing, and especially when you are starting out, it is critical that you have someone experienced next to you throughout the process.

And that brings us to the next group...

3. This last category of Canadian real estate investing experts is my favorite, the active real estate investor and "Coach".

This type of expert is on the streets with you. They are your friend, relative or mentor who is an active investor in your market. They understand the little nuances in your area that can make or break you. They are the ones who take the information and implement it.

They turn the idea into action.

They have the contacts, the know-how, the guts and the experience. They stand by you while you invest. You can call them and talk to them over long periods of time about your investments to brainstorm, problem solve and offer advice.

This is who you are looking for. The first group is great at getting you motivated and the second group of investors is good at teaching you. This last type of expert is offering real world education. And a good education based off real-world activities is priceless.

So when a new real estate investor explains that some "expert" gave them a great new idea, I always ask enough questions to find our more about the source. Which category does that expert fall into: "Eye Opener", "Traditional Expert" or "Coach".

If someone gives you a cool strategy, ask them if they've done it before in their own backyard.

If they haven't, then you know there could be some missing details. Some big details.

If they have invested successfully and are willing to stand by you through the process, lock them up! You've found a rare bird.

Now, go do something!

20
Valuable Lessons can be Taken from EVERY Experience

I just sat down at my computer and the doorbell rang. It was a sales rep that was offering me a local coupon booklet for $29.99. I am sure most people will almost regret opening the door when they realize they are about to be sold something. I actually don't mind if the person is a competent salesperson (which there seem to be few of).

Let's first understand that going door-to-door selling coupon books is not the most glamorous of jobs. I think many people I know wouldn't even have the nerve to attempt such a thing. So, I was eagerly waiting to hear the pitch.

As always, the book is being sold for a local charity (for some reason I always doubt that much of the money makes it to them), which is a way to get your guard down. The young gentleman that came to my door did a great job of introducing himself with some energy, enough to capture my attention in the first few seconds he had before I totally lost interest.

I was even offered a handshake at introduction, this has not happened to me before with a door-to-door salesperson. Some people may not like a handshake, but I am still of a traditional mindset and feel that a handshake makes a difference.

Next, he led me down a road of questions specifically designed to have me saying, 'Yes'. It's a common sales tactic taught, but there is always a difference between learning something in a classroom and implementing it in real life. This guy implemented!

The next part was subtle but executed well. He had two booklets in his hand and passed me one so he could flip the other one to a page and show me some of the most valuable coupons. As he handed it to me he said something similar to, "I only had two books left as this area you live in has been great and people are snapping them up". This was only said in passing but it is a big lesson.

No matter how we perceive it in the back of our mind, we get that funny thought: "Well, if all my neighbours have one, then maybe I should, too."

Also, it was a seamless way to put the product in my hand, for me to get the feeling of using it.

Plus, by stating that he only had two left, it made me feel that I had to act or lose out, another powerful technique. As humans, we generally want we can't have or have the risk of losing.

He did more things in the two minute transaction we had than I have seen high paid sales reps do after spending more than an hour with them.

I turned him down purposely to see what his next move would be, and it was to offer the lower priced alternative. Of course, he explained that there was not as much value, but if I only had a limited amount of cash I could just go for this alternative and still help 'the cause'.

Whether this process was crafted for or by him is irrelevant, because it is effective. If he came up with it, then he has some natural ability. If it was taught, we are back to the good implementation. How many of us are taught things that can benefit us that we never use?

I know dozens of people personally that speak of making a difference in their life and attend many types of wealth building workshops, but their rate of implementation is 0. It is what sets apart the winners and the losers in life. You can watch things go by or you can hop on the train.

In case you were wondering, I did buy from him. Not because I think I will use the product but because it was one of the better sales people I had come across in a while.

I also felt that the value for me wasn't the product, but in the sales refresher I just went through that will benefit me many times over if I, too, implement. Take note of this transaction, because it can pay dividends.

There is one regret I have as I sit down and write this: I wish I had asked him if he was looking for a new line of work!

21
"Real Estate Investing Secrets That Are Convenient To Ignore"

OK, let's just get right to it...

Real Estate Investing Secrets, Number 1. The first thing to keep in mind is that real estate investing is a local sport. So don't get caught up in the CNN headlines that say the U.S. market is collapsing. Is it suffering pretty badly? Yes, but not everywhere.

It's like me telling you that, "It's sunny in Canada today". Although that may be true in some parts of the country, it's definitely not sunny everywhere. It can be sunny in Mississauga and I'll drive 10 minutes to Oakville, and it's raining cats and dogs. Real Estate investing is the same way. You must ignore the headlines. It's mandatory.

Real Estate Investing Secrets, Number 2. You must get the data yourself, or work with people that have it. For example, with the "sky is falling" media everywhere, I decided to look at the prices in Oakville, Milton, Burlington and Hamilton for August and found prices are up in August 2008 versus August 2007 by 3-5%.

Get the data for yourself. Use local real estate boards, as they have great data. And use Census Canada data for population trends by community.

Real Estate Investing Secrets, Number 3. In good economic times, all housing increases in value. However, higher end homes spike up much higher than "starter" homes. So they are usually the ones that fall the most.

For those of you who know us, you heard us explain that our family has personal experience in this from the early 90's crash. Be aware of this. When people say house prices are falling, ask them what type of house they are talking about. Make them get specific. Don't let lazy opinions sit unchallenged.

Real Estate Investing Secrets, Number 4. In poor economic times (aside: if there even is such a thing, I know many people who just "decide" not to participate in bad times and go on to create amazing amounts of wealth while everyone else is running for cover), housing and shelter is still a need.

Read that again, housing and shelter is a need. So, if you focus your investing on categories of homes that are needed (think starter homes) you exposure to risk is much less.

Real Estate Investing Secrets, Number 5. The U.S. was giving out mortgages with no down payments to people who weren't working. Bad idea. Bad business. In Canada, we had and still have some zero down mortgages but you actually have to have good credit and a job to qualify. Big difference. Really big.

In the U.S., you can deduct mortgage insurance off your taxes, in Canada you can't. You actually have to save some money in Canada to buy a house. This is a big deal. Does it mean Canada is immune to a downturn in the real estate market? No.

You know why? Downturns are normal. They are to be expected. They are to be planned for, and to be profited from.

Real Estate Investing Secrets, Number 6. Because real estate is played locally, there are always opportunities in any market: up, down or sideways. Focus on good communities (employment diversity, growing population), think Burlington, Cambridge, Kitchener, Waterloo, even the Hamilton Mountain and Brantford in Ontario.

Real Estate Investing Secrets, Number 7. Then, focus on good houses that will produce positive cash flow for you.

Don't get stuck "flipping" a house if you can't afford to hold it for many months without an offer. Been there, and it's not fun and it's not funny. Real estate investing is very different than real estate rehabbing. The latter is more like creating a job for yourself.

Real Estate Investing Secrets, Number 8. Find a good team of people. A good team of people knows how to invest. A good team will steer you past obstacles.

We've said this before, and we'll say it again: The team is more important than the property. Remember that. Beginners forget it or don't know it. That's not you.

Real Estate Investing Secrets, Number 9. History has proven that massive amounts of wealth have been created in times of uncertainty.

Think Carnegie, Getty, Rockefeller, Trump. Rob Minton has a great report about this, and we'll touch on it later.

Real Estate Investing Secrets, Number 10. Don't buy into the hype. Think for yourself. When everyone is running one way, there is money to be made going the other way. Just the other day (September 2008), one of our investors got $13,000 up front in non-refundable money from a tenant in one of their properties.

People are making money right in your own backyard. Seriously, if you don't believe me, track down the book *Acres of Diamonds* by Russell Conwell. It's a short little story, and it'll explain everything.

Real Estate Investing Secrets, Number 11. Use these 3 steps. First, find a team of people. Second, use a proven system that others have tested. Third, get started. Read and go to seminars, but after six months, if you haven't done anything, you are wasting time. Will you make mistakes? Yes.

Will your team of professionals get you through them? Yes. Will you grow and come out stronger? Definitely.

Real Estate Investing Secrets, Number 12. Stop listening to your family and friends. Only listen to people who are doing it or have done it. Just stop listening and stop engaging in negative conversations.

Is real estate investing as simple as "colour by numbers"? No. But that's why there's money it, because not everyone will use their creativity to create wealth. You will use yours.

Real Estate Investing Secrets, Number 13. Stop sleep walking and get busy. Hustle a little. It's good for you and it's a forgotten mode of operation.

Phew, there it is, now that it's off my chest I can enjoy my day....remember, be a Renegade, always!

22
The 5 W's of Real Estate Investing Clubs

It seems with every passing day, there are more real estate investing clubs starting up. Overall, this is great, because it is important to **get the word out that you can have great success investing in real estate**.

But with all these options out there, where do you turn?

Over time, we have attended meetings or have been members of many different real estate investing clubs and have been able to gather some **good and bad** pointers

Here are the **5 W's** you should know:

1. **Why the Hype?** – Some of these clubs may have flashy meetings or presentations, but you might want to ask yourself what is going on **behind the smoke and mirrors?** Often a big production will be put on to generate some emotion and get you all pumped up to act on something. Sometimes it can be thousands of dollars in training.

    Now let me clarify: I am not saying that whatever training is being offered is bad, but just be sure that you **know what you are getting into** and don't just act strictly on the hype in the room.

    I recently met an extremely nice lady who bought into the hype. She and her husband **invested $10 000** in courses with one of the popular real estate investing clubs, only to have her **course rescheduled, and then cancelled**.

    As much as she tried, she was unable to secure a refund for the money she put out. Now, this doesn't mean that there aren't some great courses or offerings out there because there are, but make sure you are **buying the value in the information** being presented not the hype.

2. **Who's Running This Thing?** – With all the groups popping up around every corner, it might be wise to have an understanding of who is leading the pack you belong to.

You might want to ask yourself if this person has actual **investment experience** themselves, or do they just talk the talk?

Advice and information are great but if they come from **real life knowledge and experience, they are more likely the real deal.** Unfortunately, the majority of people are only out for their bottom line and that can lead to some inaccurate information being tossed around.

You want to be learning from people who are making things happen. Ideally, they would be **investors themselves.** That way, you can leverage the life lessons they have encountered. It is amazing what you can learn in your first few investments. Learn from the people that have been through it and can share their mistakes, so you can avoid them.

3. **What's The Big Picture?** – Yes there are many benefits to working within real estate investing clubs, but I am not sure that any single one of them is doing it out of the kindness of their hearts.

There is something in it for them. And to be clear that is great!

Everyone has to make a living or a profit -- there is absolutely no problem with that. But it is nice to have an understanding of what is in it for them, so you can make proper, informed decisions when listening to their advice or presentations. For example, when you go to Wal Mart to buy a TV, you know what the deal is. They offer you the TV at a price that helps you save some money, but at the same time allows them to make money as well. **Perfect! That is a win win scenario.** Make sure that you are getting involved in the same.

The relationship shouldn't be you giving without getting anything in return.

4. **Where's the Beef?** – Yeah, you are right. It's an interesting question when talking about real estate investing clubs, but I think it gets the point across.

   Is there substance to what is preached? **Motivational talks are fun** and leave you with a great feeling, but you want to **look for solid information**. That is what is going to make you successful.

   Are there **proven techniques and strategies** that are being taught, or is your club just feeding you fluff? If you are going to invest your time reading and attending meetings, don't you want them to be worthwhile? It might be beneficial to **take a step back** and make sure that there is some real information being provided, and if implemented, can get you on the track to success or speed up your trip a bit.

5. **When Will I Use This?** – This is a big one, but may depend more on you than the club. It involves **taking the next step**.

   Are you going to **use the information** and methods that you gather, or are you going to analyze it forever while jumping around from group to group for the next hot topic?

   Really think about this. If you are not going to start implementing this information, why are you spending your time on it? **The right Real Estate investing clubs are for everyone,** but if you are not going to use what is given to you, it may not be the best use of your time.

As some other markets continue to slow and ours keeps moving up, there are going to be more and more 'clubs' starting up. Some of them may be the real deal, but I can promise you some of them won't be.

Be sure to look at them closely and decide which is the right one for you.

23
Buying Investment Real Estate Requires the Proper Mindset

I've written about the mindset required when buying investment real estate in the past, and it always creates a bunch of questions.

One of the first blog posts we posted started a discussion in our office.

I'll summarize it like this:

1. You want to do something new...like invest in real estate.
2. You feel overwhelmed by all the things you don't know but think you should.
3. This causes a fear of failure
4. You ultimately don't want to be called a failure and be judged by your peers, so you PROCRASTINATE.

I mentioned in my previous post on this that the book by Neil Fiore, PhD, titled *The Now Habit* is by far the best resource for explaining the reasons why people procrastinate that I've ever come across. I highly recommend it.

So, a bunch of people started asking about why we get that initial overwhelming feeling that seems to cause all the problems.

Again, I'll have to refer back to Neil's book that provides some great insights.

And after working with MANY investors, I can share from first hand experiences that his thoughts on this seem amazingly accurate.

Here goes...

The feeling of overwhelm that a beginner gets when thinking of buying investment real estate initially comes from **insisting on the right place to start**.

When buying investment real estate, especially when buying it for the first time, people often spend tremendous amounts of time scrambling for the perfect place to start.

Is it a single family home, a condo, a property under $300,000, over $300,000, downtown, in the burbs, a condo conversion project, a flip, new construction? And the list goes on and on.

What most people buying investment real estate don't understand is that your path to wealth is not a linear one.

All of these may be the right choices, given the right mentor and education.

What you really need to do is begin.

By beginning with ANY of the possible investments, you build a base of experience that you can learn from and make even better decisions based on in the future.

But without that base of experience to lean on, you have nothing.

So initially, it's more important to find a mentor, get some education (six months of reading is more than enough) and then taking action.

You are building your base of experience by taking the first step, and that's almost more important than the investment itself.

OK, here's the next part...

When beginners start buying investment real estate, they typically **don't allow themselves the time to develop their confidence**.

They want to be perfect at negotiating the lease, picking the property, collecting cash and they want to be perfect at it right now.

This is wrong, and builds that feeling of overwhelm.

When buying investment real estate, you need to learn as you go. Each step in the process of finding a home, negotiating to purchase it, closing on it, renting it out and making a profit from it is part of the process.

And, if you've never done any of the steps before, you will make some mistakes. It's those mistakes that build your experience and make you better at it.

So, you must expect some mistakes. You must ask for help. You must give yourself permission to be less than perfect.

This attitude will go a long way in making the process of buying investment real estate bearable for you.

And now for the last part...

I see this one almost all the time with beginners buying investment real estate.

They will think that they need to be "finished already". Neil Fiore has really hit the nail on the head with this one.

Often, beginners won't accept that they are "not finished already". They didn't get the tenant they wanted for their first property during week one and they get discouraged.

They get frustrated with their level of accomplishment at the beginning and compare it with the "ideal" they set out with at the beginning.

See most people just focus on the end, in the case having a property rented, and not the process.

So when they begin showing their property and don't get it rented out immediately, they begin to freak out because they only saw the finish line and forgot about the journey.

And this leads to a massive feeling of overwhelm and stress.

The above observations can be applied to almost anything. Neil Fiore has done an amazing job with the book and for the second time I'll throw out a strong recommendation for it.

24
"Your Education in Real Estate Investing Must Include Fire Fighting...and Yes, We're Serious!"

Look, when getting your education in real estate investing, there's something you need to know.

It's great to read about real estate investing. And it's wonderful to teach yourself about the proper mindset required to "attract" success.

But to really get rolling, you need to combine the proper mindset with action. It's that combination that propels you towards your goals faster than either one alone.

But you've probably heard all that before, so let me throw something else into the mix here. Let me spice up your education in real estate investing.

Once you get into action, you need to be able to handle the heat.

Most people run from it. Most people don't want to feel pressure. Most people don't want to be stressed. Most people don't want to battle their way through problems. Most people want to run and hide at the first sight of a challenge.

And most people aren't living the life they desire. Go figure.

Here's what I mean about being able to handle the heat.

Invariably, when you invest in real estate, you will hit hiccups along the way. The insurance company will make you do back flips to confirm the certification of the heating or the old wood burning fireplace. And the cash flow you projected for the first 12 months may get eaten up by an unexpected repair.

Or the tenants you thought would stay for 24 months decide to move out after 12...leaving you scrambling to find a replacement. Or maybe it takes you longer to rent the property than you planned in your "cash flow" spreadsheet.

Well, it's how you handle these events that determine if you've got what it takes to be a successful investor.

Because, if you decide to sell the property or if you decide to bail at the first sign of imperfection -- you are acting like the majority. And the majority of people is not the group you want to be part of.

It's the tough times, the handling of unexpected events and difficult people that separate you from the masses.

And things that most people avoid (pressure, stress, fear) are the very things that make you stronger. They are the things that people who reach their goals battle through.

This is what your education in real estate investing should focus on!

In nature, it's normal for seasons to change and it's normal for major chaotic transformations to occur. This is going to sound a little ridiculous, but a caterpillar only turns into a butterfly by going through some pretty serious transformations. The most perfect day almost always follows a terrible storm.

Handling problems and issues and sticking through things is the transformational process that will build your confidence and make you stronger.

And with an increase in confidence, you handle bigger problems and with bigger problems come bigger rewards.

I'm speaking from direct experience here.

If you are having trouble battling through a current problem or decision you are facing, I have an exercise for you.

Let's keep this on topic and focus your education in real estate investing on a real life situation.

Let's say you are about to make your first investment.

And let's assume that you are scared of failing. You are scared of losing money, being judged and being declared a laughing stock. You know, the typical stuff.

In order to push through all that, you need some motivation.

Here's the education in real estate investing exercise. It's the plank test that I first came across in a book by Neil Fiore, *The Now Habit*.

Step 1: Imagine a ten foot plank on the ground that's two feet wide. Could you walk across it? Yes, absolutely.

Step 2: Now, imagine that same plank 100 feet in the air, acting as a bridge between two building tops. Could you walk across it then? Maybe, but it's a lot harder, right?

Why is it a lot harder? It's because you are focusing on the fall, on the fear of failing. You're not focusing on how easy the task at hand really is.

This is what most people do when they think of real estate investing. They focus on the potential of losing money, the potential of failure, the potential of humiliation by their family and peers if they fail.

Now let's move to the next step:

Step 3: Now, imagine a huge roaring fire behind you that is going to burn you alive unless you get across that plank, pronto. Could you do it then? Yeah, probably in the blink of an eye.

So let me leave you with this. What's your burning fire? What is going to give you the kick in the a$$ that you need to get moving?

If you don't have your fire, go off and light one up. Today.

25
A Real Estate Investing Program Works *IF* You Don't Quit Like Everyone Else

Most people never finish a Real Estate Investing Program once they start. By "program", I mean any organized plan to invest in real estate.

I'm not really sure why people give up too early, but it's a common pattern that we're all guilty of.

The art of patience and self discipline seems to have disappeared from the psyche of the masses. Not really sure why, but everywhere I turn, people want the quick fix, the quick cash, the quick wealth.

This obsession with "quick" is a fatal flaw.

Let me relate this as best I can to a real estate investing program. A client we work with had a goal to buy six properties in one year. And another had no real goal, but just wanted to get started and make money with real estate investing.

The first client made six offers and lost out on every single one before getting his first property.

The second client made an offer on one property, lost out on it and gave up on the real estate investing program all together. Totally gave up after not winning his first offer.

The first client, now (9 months later) owns six properties, all producing positive cash flow.

The second client has no properties (we no longer work with him so I could be wrong, but I doubt he has any, and I would be happy to be proven wrong).

The first client's net worth (according to my rough calculations based on appreciation of 8% that occurred in the area) has increased by $50,000. And that's just this past 9 months. With the positive cash flow, immediate cash extraction, tax write-offs and equity build-up in the property, it could be more. And the real wealth will build not now, but over the next several years.

Why does one person quit while the next person continues on?

I've been obsessed with this question. And I think the answer lies mainly in each person's maturity level. At a certain point, you just realize that you have to put in consistent, focused work to reap any rewards.

Early in a person's "wealth building" cycle, they are too scattered. Always looking for the next big thing. Always looking for the next best real estate investing program. They go from wanting to flip, to rent, to apartment buildings, to land development, to nothing.

I think that's why many people run around like chickens with their head cut off, from one boot camp to another seminar, to the next networking event. When you're always striving for the next big thing, you don't focus long enough to achieve anything.

Achieving your goals isn't very complicated, but I guess keeping focused is. It's a challenge for me.

This chapter is inspired by something I read in one of Robin Sharma's books, *The Greatness Guide*.

In it, he writes, "Consistency. It's amazing how far you will get by just staying with something long enough."

This is true for a real estate investing program and for everything.

A while back, I was a sales manager at a software company as it was going public on the New York Stock Exchange (NYSE).

Most sales reps would join and if they didn't have immediate success, would give up. But there was this one guy who really struggled out of the gates. He didn't hit his monthly, quarterly or yearly quotas. Not even close. And I even asked him if this was the right field of work for him.

Now, most people would get discouraged if your sales manager was trying to talk you out of your job, but he didn't bite. He just kept working and working and working. Today, he's one of the top two sales reps in the entire division.

Now, I don't mean any disrespect to him, but his sales talent was average at best.

But his ability to stay consistent and to keep working was ABOVE AVERAGE.

This is an important lesson. His skills were below average, but it didn't really matter, because he consistently kept at his goal.

And I've learned that being consistent is more important than being talented.

We all know talented people not living up to their potential.

But I bet you don't know many people who stick with their goal through thick and thin.

It's easy to give up during the lull period before you hit success. I think the key to achieving anything you want is realizing that once the initial enthusiasm of your quest wears off, it's critical to keep with it and fight your way through the lull we all experience just before success.

Let me be clear. I've read about the concept of "fighting on until you hit success" for years, but never really understood it until about four or five years ago.

Now I know the pattern. I know that just when my enthusiasm cools on a new idea, if at that exact time, I press on anyway, I will hit the goal. I almost watch for the "lull" now. Because I know it's at that point I am so close to success. It's at that point that I know if I just buckle down and press on, I will win the day.

And you how I came to understand this?

I finally didn't quit a new challenge. I stuck with it and battled on. The confidence that I now have, knowing that I can achieve almost anything that I put my mind to is invaluable to me.

As you've read elsewhere in this book, don't follow the masses and quit too early.

Success in anything you want (even in a real estate investing program) is really pretty simple.

What goal have you not achieved lately? Did you stay with it long enough? I doubt it.

Press on.

26
Real Estate Investment Book "Income For Life for Canadians" And a BIG LESSON!

You know when we first talked about putting this real estate investment book together, we really had no idea what we were getting ourselves into.

But it's finally done! And I want to share a story about it with you.

The day after we picked up the first batch of them, hot off the printers presses, we threw them in the trunk of my car and hauled them into the member event we were holding the next day.

Now we had no clue that we would actually be handing these things out, but before we knew it, we were selling them and a dozen were out the door before we could blink.

Two days later, we received an email from one of our members stating that the real estate investment book was all messed up.

Now we know we're not Mark Twain, but our real estate investment book was by no means "all messed up"!

So we looked into it and found that a bunch of the pages were out of order.

At this point, we could have gone down two paths:

1. Panic.

2. Act and move on.

We chose option #2.

We called the printer, and to his credit, he agreed to fix it all for no cost. If anyone needs the name of a good printer in the Toronto area, send me a note! Most vendors I've dealt with will kick and scream and not do the right thing, but he acted quickly and now has a customer for life.

But here's the bigger lesson in this...

When this issue popped up, all of sudden we had everyone looking at the real estate investment book for spelling mistakes, typos and any other errors. And a few did some.

We ignored the mistakes and reprinted the book quickly without fixing them.

And a lot of people couldn't understand why we would have done that. Shouldn't we have waited until it was proof read to perfection?

NO!

That's how most people do things. And I'm sure enough kind people will gladly point out every mistake for us...basically acting as our proof readers for free. Cool eh?

From my experience, the masses are perfectionists with things that don't make them money. Especially beginners at real estate investing.

They won't advertise their property until the hairline scratch on the wall is touched up, or the driveway is cleared of snow or the hole in the closet is patched up perfectly.

See? There's a little secret to making money that is often overlooked.

You don't need to get things perfect -- you just need to get things going.

So with the book, we knew it was more important to get it printed and get it out there than have the website setup, the 16th proof read completed, and our pictures have the right sunlight to shadow ratio. That stuff doesn't make us money.

But getting the book out into the hands of people does.

Now you need to have the majority of things in place, but waiting until you hang the perfect picture in the family room before you advertise the property is often a waste of time.

Getting people to the property makes you money. And if you do it in the right way, you can literally have holes in the walls and get it rented out. We have.

The next time you find yourself fretting over something, the best advice we can offer is get over it and get moving.

If you stand on the sidelines and try to figure out every single detail of investing in real estate before you take any action, you'll likely not get very far.

You need to figure things out as you go. And if you have a good mentor by your side, things will work out just fine.

All the big achievers I know just plow ahead, and as problems arise, they act on them and move on.

Analysis paralysis doesn't put money into your bank account.

If you'd like a copy of the notorious book, please drop us a line.

27
Investing In Commercial Real Estate - Is the Grass Always Greener? Maybe.

Investing in commercial real estate is a huge topic that has a ton of great angles.

We deal exclusively with investors and focus a lot of time and energy into residential real estate investing. And just being in this line of work regularly leads to discussions around commercial investing.

Commercial investing (think apartment buildings, strip malls and town house complexes etc.) has many differences to that of residential investing.

Around financing, there are things like larger down payments, more expensive inspections (including environmental assessments), mortgage broker fees, slightly higher mortgage rates, and property managers.

Many new investors figure there's a lot of money in larger commercial investments just because they are larger than residential investments.

Now this may be the case, but there are a few things to think about.

The down payment required is going to be 25%. So, if you're looking at a $4,000,000 building, you need to pony up $1,000,000 to purchase it.

Or, on a smaller scale, if you go for a $1,000,000 six-plex in the out skirts of the Greater Toronto Area, you need $250,000.

With $250,000, you can acquire over $2,000,000 in residential investments with the newly minted mortgage programs for investors. So you can definitely "leverage up" with residential more easily than with commercial.

Investing in commercial real estate may be more "passive". Isn't that everyone's goal? Lie on the beach while the cheques roll in, right? Well, I can tell you that there's nothing that is truly passive in real estate.

Commercial buildings with property management may be more passive than residential, but they're definitely not 100% hands-free. And, if you treat them like that, your property manager will likely be making more money from the venture than you do.

And the expected capitalization rate in the Greater Toronto area when investing in commercial real estate is around 8%.

Another thing to be aware of, but regularly overlooked, is the valuations.

Canadian commercial investment properties are valued according to the revenue/income that they generate.

Residential investment properties are typically valued according to comparable properties on the street.

So, if you are renting out a single family home and the other homes in the area appreciate, your property typically appreciates along with them. Recently, that's been a very healthy rate.

The downside, of course, is that if the market falls for homes on your street, then your investment property goes down with the rest (remember, think long term and don't let the short thinking masses who are often distracted by shiny objects get to you).

Investing in commercial real estate usually doesn't have this issue, because again, the value of commercial investment properties are more closely tied to the rent they generate and because that fluctuates less, the value of the properties fluctuates less.

So when you are looking to build wealth investing, commercial real estate has its place, but it's not the silver bullet you may think it is.

The wealthiest investors will look at commercial investing the same way we look at residential investing. Find a deal, lock it up, and profit from it.

Canadian commercial real estate "deals" are properties that are mismanaged, and can be acquired for less than market value because the rents are low. They are then turned around quickly by raising rents with a better management team.

Investing in commercial real estate has the same basic fundamentals of any types of investments.

In my opinion, there's one common mistake that many beginners getting started investing in commercial real estate make.

They'll go off and buy an 8-plex because they believe that if one of the units goes vacant, they have 7 other units generating cash for them.

And if they're investing in a single family home, and the tenants leave, they have no other income stream.

Here's some insight on this thought.

Basically, the quality of a property is directly tied to the quality of its tenants. A family renting out a single family home may be more stable than bachelors renting out units in an 8-plex.

So, if I own several single family homes, purchase them wisely, and manage them smartly, a pool of three or four nice single family homes in good areas spread out my risk more than a single 8-plex. Of course, this is just an opinion.

To wrap this up, there's no one right answer. For some, residential investing is the key to their success. For others, it's investing in commercial real estate.

Your journey will likely involve both at some point. As with everything, there's no one single right answer.

Focus on your long term goals and then make decisions accordingly.

There are specific strategies to make big bucks investing in commercial real estate.

We'll discuss it in another time, but it's more along the lines of commercial development and is definitely an active, not passive, process.

28
The Top 10 Real Estate Investing FAQ List - Part 1

It can be hard to decipher all the information out there. So to help, here is The Top 10 Real Estate Investing FAQ List.

Many investors I have spoken with are looking for the answers to some of the basic questions, so the thought of putting them all in one place just seemed to make sense, right?

This wasn't supposed to be a **two part article,** but after starting the list, there was just TOO much information for one article -- so it had to be split up!

Let's go!

Real Estate Investing FAQ Question 1 - When should I get started?

I figured we would start with an easy one .-)

The answer is **"Right Now"**.

There is no better time to start.

With each passing day, you are missing out on potential profits to be made. There is **a ton of opportunity** in many different Canadian markets and all over the U.S. (Yes, even with what you hear on CNN).

The key to remember is to gather the facts on the market and type of investment you are looking to get into. But, with the most common approach of 'Buy and Hold', there is no reason to wait - you have to get yourself into the game.

There is **money being made every single day in real estate**. You have to decide if you want to be part of that or continue talk yourself out of it.

Real Estate Investing FAQ Question 2 - Is Real Estate Really A Good Investment?

It may best to use a **real life example** for this one.

One of the investments I own is a student rental By McMaster University in Hamilton, ON.

I purchased this home as a power of sale a few years ago with a friend. And although he was extremely hesitant at the time, I knew a **cash cow** when I saw one.

We did do some major renovations to this house. I forget the exact number, but I know we spent more than we wanted to!

After all was said and done, we were able to refinance the property and get ALL the money we spent on renovations plus our down payment back.

Did you catch that?

We now owned the house and every penny that we had taken out of our pocket to buy and fix it was now back in our hands!!

That's big, but wait, **it gets better**.

On top of the money that we had invested into the property, we were also able to take a few thousand dollars each as profit.

Not big money, but in the matter of a few months, it is definitely worth noting.

Plus, the home was still worth more than the mortgage on it. So we still had extra profit (as equity) sitting in the home because **we STILL OWNED IT**.

Now it was time to rent it out, as the school year was approaching. We did that, and even after the refinance we were **making about $700 a month in positive cash flow**.

So, just to bring this all together...

I now owned a property that I no longer had money invested in, it was worth tens of thousands of dollars more than the mortgage on it, and it was making $700 a month in positive cash flow.

So from this, the **answer** to real estate investing faq number 2 is a resounding **"YES, yes, and yes!"**

Real Estate Investing FAQ Question 3 - What Is The Best Type of Real Estate to Invest In?

This is a tough one, because there are so many good investments available. But it is a common question and deserves a spot on the real estate investing FAQ list.

Ultimately, it comes down to your long term goals and risk level.

Yes, I just used a four letter word **"R I S K"**

There is always risk involved in investing, and you have probably heard the old saying **"No Risk No Reward".** Well I've got news for you, it's true.

The key is to *collect enough information so that you can minimize your risk*. But we will come to that, let's stick with the question.

Let's use vacant land as an example.

Vacant land can pay **massive returns,** but there are not too many people that have the finances to purchase large areas of land or the expertise to know how to extract profit through development.

There can also be some big hiccups along the way. For anyone in Ontario, you may remember when the Ontario government decided to protect the Greenbelt, which essentially stopped all development in those areas.

Now, if you were an investor with some land there, that can be a good sized hiccup.

So although vacant land can hold some excellent opportunity, you have to be a certain type of investor to maximize those returns.

Most beginner investors will invest in some sort of residential real estate. It could be a single family home or maybe a small building with 3 or 4 units.

Residential investments are easier to get into.

Usually, there is **less capital** required to get into the game (which is important, remember real estate investing FAQ 1?) and your turn around time to see some profit or benefits is much quicker.

Focusing on your strengths, your risk tolerance, and your financial situation should give you an idea of what the best type of real estate investment is for you.

Educate yourself and set realistic expectations of your investment. Just like not every stock or bond is for every person, the same can be said for real estate.

In my personal opinion, if you are a beginner just getting started, you may want to investigate the residential side of investments first.

The thing to remember when answering real estate investing FAQ number 3 is that there is definitely at least one type of real estate investment that fits your needs, so be sure to **find it and then do it!**

Real Estate Investing FAQ Question 4 - What About Paying Taxes?

If only I charged for my time whenever I have explained how my tax situation works!

Taxes are complicated.

Taxes in Canada are even **MORE complicated.**

I use an accountant that is either an angel or a rock star depending on how you want to look at him. He's likely both rolled into one.

I can not stress enough that if you are investing in real estate, you must use an accountant that knows real estate specifically. You are leaving money on the table if you are not.

Many people will try to cut corners because it costs money to use a professional, but my experiences have taught me that paying the money will pay **large dividends** back to you.

My tax situation has a lot of moving parts, and because of that, I was reassessed by the Canadian government in 2006.

The peace of mind *alone* to be able to forward that paperwork off and let my accountant take care of it was worth the investment.

And that's how you need to look at it: an **accountant is an investment** into your real estate investment business -- no matter big or small.

I am going to refrain from giving any **specific tax advice,** since I am not qualified and someone reading this that does not take responsibility for his own actions will try to **hold me liable!!**

I will tell you that there are **definite and absolute tax benefits** to investing in real estate.

There are reasons why wealthy individuals all invest in real estate in one way or another. Yes, there is money to be made on the real estate itself, but there are also huge tax benefits.

While thinking about the answer to real estate investing FAQ number 4, this comes to mind...

<u>I have always been able to keep more of the money I made from real estate investments than any job that I have ever had.</u>

Don't forget I live in Canada, where we are world famous for our high taxes...**OUCH!!**

But if there is a way to make money and pay fewer taxes, then I'm all over it.

Real Estate Investing FAQ Question 5 - What If My Investment Doesn't Go as Planned?

This is a very common question. And the most blunt answer I can give is **'It Probably Won't'**.

Only rarely do the stars align and everything goes exactly as you had envisioned before setting out on your journey.

You should look at realistic worst-case scenarios to see if you are comfortable with them.

If I owned a rental property, I know that somehow, someway, it IS possible that a gaping hole opens up in the Earth and the home is swallowed up.

Is that realistic? **NO.**

But you wouldn't believe the things I hear from people too scared to get into the game (again, remember real estate investing FAQ 1 -- it's a big one!).

A more realistic scenario is that the property doesn't get rented out in the time you think it will.

And again, **we have to be realistic**. One week is not a typical time frame to rent out a property.

This is probably the beginner investor's biggest fear when first investing in real estate.

"My plan is to rent out the property, but what if..?"

You get the idea.

This is something that should be addressed before you buy the property.

There are some **questions to ask yourself** in addition to the real estate investing FAQ questions:

1. Is the property nice enough for someone to live in it?
2. Is it nice enough for people to genuinely be attracted to the place when they walk through the door?
3. Are other people in the area getting the same type of payment that you are expecting to get?
4. What is my plan to get someone into the home?

These are the questions that you should be asking yourself ahead of time, so that you have an idea if your plan is realistic.

In this specific example, the worst case is that you'll have to lower the rent if you don't rent it out. Remember, there are always tenants looking for nice places to live.

Account for that in your planning. If you have to drop the rent $100 per month how does that change things?

1. Will you still get appreciation?
2. Will you still get tax benefits?
3. Will you still get all or most of your mortgage payment, and property taxes covered?

If you look at the **big picture,** is this still a very worthwhile investment?

It will be difficult to find a case where it is not - especially if you are honest with yourself at the beginning.

Things will rarely go as planned, but account for the hurdles and **have a plan**.

The experiences of overcoming these hurdles are what investing is all about. It's what life is all about.

They will make you a stronger person, and looking back, those hurdles will become small pebbles that, in the future, you will walk right over. And that is where the fun begins, because **bigger hurdles mean bigger rewards.**

We are halfway through our Top Ten Real Estate Investing FAQ list and it has been fun so far.

I can't believe how this list has grown. I think I was expecting the real estate investing FAQ answers to be short and sweet.

Stay Tuned for Part 2...Same Renegade time, Same Renegade channel...

29
"Creative Real Estate Investing May Be Bad For Your Long Term Success"

What do creative real estate investing and U2 have in common?

Check this out...

I was reading something from Perry Marshall the other day that made me laugh out loud. Perry is a marketing guy and he comes up with some fantastic content. I'm going to use a similar analogy he shared and tie it to real estate investing here...

Have you ever noticed how some things just stand the test of time?

For example, a great rock song from U2 fifteen years ago is just as good or even better today. You've learned to appreciate the song and it just has a pureness to it.

Even the real hard stuff like AC/DC *Thunderstruck* gets your juices flowing today even more today than when you first heard it.

On the flip side, notice how the latest Britney song or Backstreet beat or New Kid lyrics are white hot when they first come out? They end up on every radio station all the time. You even find yourself tapping the steering wheel to the beat.

But then it fades, and it fades fast.

A year later, if that song comes on, you almost cringe. You can't believe you actually liked that song.

Has this ever happened to you?

Well, the same thing happens in a person's journey along the real estate investing path.

Let's map it out and tie creative real estate investing into this...

1. You decide you are fed up with your 9-5 job and you need to get out -- quick.

2. You see an American TV infomercial on at 2a.m. (because you're dreading Monday morning and you can't sleep). You ask yourself if this creative real estate investing stuff is your ticket out of the rat race. But then you ask, can it work for Canadians too?

3. You hit the local Chapters book store on your lunch break and pick up a book about real estate investing. Maybe it's *Rich Dad, Poor Dad* or *The Millionaire Next Door* or *The Wealthy Barber*. The ideas seem sound, so you start looking around for anyone doing it.

4. You begin to notice a lot of weekend book camps and investor meetings with some guy at the front giving a hard pitch for you to part ways with $10,000 to get some creative real estate investing training. You actually debate doing it, but something deep inside you is screaming. It just doesn't feel right.

5. You think back to those books you read and realize that there's definitely some truth to real estate investing. But who can help you?

6. And that's where it usually ends. An endless loop of you going to countless investor meetings, where a lot of creative real estate investing hype is happening but no real results. A lot of "lucrative" deals are discussed, but no details are given -- unless you pass through the gates that require thousands of bucks as an entrance fee.

7. You begin to get frustrated and either give up or strike out on your own trying to do a "flip" because it looks so sexy on TV. If the guys on TLC and A&E can do it, so can you, right?

8. You hit a couple of road bumps with the mortgage and the contractors. You don't have anyone to turn to, and all of a sudden your dream of becoming Mr. or Ms. Donald Trump II fades as fast as those lyrics to that Britney song.

Yeah, been there!

It took us a long time to understand some basic principles in real estate investing.

Perhaps they can benefit you, so let me share:

Principle #1: Real estate investing is very different than "flipping" or "rehabbing" or "very wacky creative real estate investing". One is a very sophisticated process, the other is speculation. One is creating a long term asset base that will feed you for years. The other is creating a job for yourself.

Principle #2: Positive cash flow investments are always better than negative cash flow investments. Always. No matter how "lucrative" the opportunity is or how "up and coming" an area is.

Principle #3: The team of people associated with the investment is more important than the investment itself. Always. Period. End of story.

Principle #4: A long term view is mandatory. The poor think day to day, the middle class think month to month, the rich think decade to decade (check out Keith Cameron Smith's book on Amazon.com before it goes out of print).

Principle #5: The numbers don't lie. But the interpretation of the numbers is equally important.

When you stick with the basics of real estate investing, everything else sort of melts away.

Basics, like fundamentally good neighborhoods and fundamentally good properties are the building blocks of a great portfolio.

It can be tough, but always try to peel the curtain back and look beyond the hype.

The team of people you associate yourself with is more important than "the deal". Remember that. And look to build your own team of experts in your community.

The other day, we had someone run into our office with an opportunity that we had to buy immediately in order to make $5,000. And if we didn't "act fast", he was going to present this deal to someone else.

A few questions about the numbers and the team of people involved scared him off. We've never seen him again. Maybe he's running his own creative real estate investing class now, who knows!

And maybe he'll be back, but just like that New Kid song that I can't remember from the 90's...I'll bet we never hear from him again!

Until next time...be a Renegade!

30
Advice for Canadian Real Estate Investors from George Ross

Any Canadian real estate investors out there not know who **George Ross** is?

He's Donald Trump's right hand man and his "go to" lawyer, who handles many of Trump's legal activities still today.

We had the opportunity to spend some time with him and hear a live chat he gave that seemed to be pretty spontaneous in its content.

We even snapped a couple of pictures with him.

One of the most interesting stories he shared was how you can never lose focus when negotiating a deal. He was down south somewhere and someone was trying to sell his wife a blanket for $30 on the beach and he offered $12.

This goes with his #1 piece of advice and magic phrase he uses in all negotiations, "You've got to do better."

Based on the sheer amount of time he spent explaining the power of that line, it's obvious he's used it very successfully over the last few decades with Trump.

I'm sure Canadian real estate investors can do the same. I've been testing it out lately with everything and it works. The dry cleaners gave me a 15% discount just for blurting it out (I was smiling as I said it).

Anyway, he spends a full day going back and forth with the beach blanket guy and ultimately lets the deal fall away over 50 cents. The guy selling the blanket came down to $15 but George's final offer was $14.50.

He explained how he regretted losing that blanket and blames it on his lack of focus.

He was more interested in "winning" and not giving up that last 50 cents than actually getting the blanket for his wife, which was the actual goal of the process.

Here are few other little gems for Canadian real estate investors that George shared:

1. Always find common ground when negotiating. If the guy on the other side of the table plays golf, then you love golf.

2. You must do your homework. Knowledge is key in complex negotiations.

3. Ability to organize information is a critical component to his success. He shared how, when he started with Donald Trump, he noticed that Donald kept a spiral notebook on his desk to track everything. He immediately started doing the same.

And I'm sure Canadian real estate investors will love this little quote he put out there:

"More fortunes have been lost in real estate than ever made".

Good one eh?

He went on to explain how a lot of people buy into things because of the "aura of legitimacy" surrounding the deals.

The specific example used was around the condo hotels in Las Vegas and how, over the past few years (2005-2008), a bunch of beginner real estate inventors bought up condo hotel units thinking that they were a slam dunk investment.

Apparently, the fine print of these things didn't guarantee the rental income that the investors believed was theirs, and now a boat load of people are carrying negative cash flow condo hotel units that aren't appreciating at the moment.

After issuing that story, he went on to explain how everyone, including Canadian real estate investors, should borrow to the hilt BUT invest in wisely.

George went on to explain that Donald Trump was buying when EVERYONE ELSE WAS SELLING.

So basically, Trump made a boat load of money by being a contrarian.

Before George goes into any negotiation, he uses his POST strategy.

P - Who are the people and personalities at the meeting.

O - What is the objective of this meeting and it must be measurable.

S – Strategy: which one? Smart/stupid/rich/poor

T – Tactics: which one? e.g. don't appear anxious.

He also made a comment on how people believe generalities instead of specifics.

That explains why everyone lives and dies by the media's headlines that the sky is falling, but overlooks the fact that one block has rising prices and another has declining ones. Very few people research and use the specifics to their advantage. Including most Canadian real estate investors I know.

Couple of last points...

George Ross handles all of Trump's licensing deals. Things like the licensing of his name for the suits that Macy's sells.

Trump surrounds himself with professionals and has supreme confidence.

This whole "supreme confidence" concept seems to be a recurring theme between huge money makers. Bill Gates and Larry Ellison (Oracle Corp.) come to mind.

I'm certain all Canadian real estate investors would benefit from the same attitude. I find that beginners often feel that everyone else knows more than they do, and it scares them from taking action.

It took me a while to figure this out, but here's a little secret for ya: hardly anyone out there knows anything and there are very few people actually taking any action. Once you come to understand that, the world is your oyster. Seriously.

George ends his talk with how important his magical phrase, "You've got to do better" has been to him.

Years ago, there was an apartment listed for $3.8 million. The seller wanted only firm offers. The developer that he was working with at the time (not Trump) wanted George to write up a firm offer for $3.4 million. Instead, George offered $1.9 million and got it for $2.4 million.

Not bad eh?

Overall, a great guy, surprisingly approachable and obviously a fountain of knowledge.

31
"Your Investment in Rental Property Should Include This Line of Thinking"

Your investment in rental property should include this line of thinking. This might sound a bit harsh, and I go off topic a bit at the start, but hear me out. I promise there is a great lesson in this.

In business, it is important to understand your costs and your return on investment. I think that is fairly simple. But it seems that many people just have not clued in yet.

Recently, I ran an ad in the local paper by our offices. This is a company and ad rep that I have spent tens of thousands of dollars with in under two years. For the first time since I started working with this company, they ran the ad without my final approval.

I am not an overly picky customer, so I would have been fine with it EXCEPT they made changes to the ad that I didn't ask for. So I have now paid for an ad (just over $600) that is not what I had requested, and I wasn't given the final say on the changes.

Now, I have never been in advertising sales, but what I can say is that I have placed many ads with a lot of different companies. And I'll let you guess what the one constant thing is...right -- they all send you a proof before the ad runs to make sure you are happy with it. I even get this service with a $100 classified ad if I ask for it.

So, I decided to call and mention that I was not sent a final proof of the ad for approval, and changes that were not requested were made. I was not angry, but I felt that there should some sort of recourse for such an incident. Really, I thought this would be a small thing that we would get resolved and move forward...it wasn't!

I will keep it short for our purposes, but by the end of it, I was in contact with the Advertising Director at the paper. And after a couple of emails which he did not even acknowledge, stating that they ran an incorrect ad, or answer any questions posed to him, he finally called me. His tone was harsh and condescending, but he grudgingly agreed to a 50% refund (which works out to be about $300 + tax).

It sounds good, but the only problem is that now I am left with an entirely different outlook on the company as a whole, and it persuades me not to do business with them any longer.

Let's look at this, because it applies directly to business and any investment in rental property.

Let's guess that I have only spent $15,000 with this company, and up until this point, was happy with everything. Because of the way I was treated for their mistake (which they did not verbally accept responsibility for) I am now left with a bad taste in my mouth. All because of the $300 I had asked for.

If handled correctly, this could have been the best $300 they ever spent. If that's what it took to keep me happy and spend another $15,000, that would be a 5000% return on their investment in less than two years. Did you catch that? 5000%!

Would you be willing to spend $300 to have a customer with a proven track record that shows that kind of return?

I would everyday of the week, and do it happily. And so would any other smart business owner.

The problem is that this advertising director didn't understand the long term value of customer, or the big picture of a business relationship.

It is sad but true. Think about the owner of the paper, who just lost out on this future revenue. He or she must be thrilled right? Nope!

How does this apply to investment in rental property? Good question.

The same principle applies. You should be looking at your potential tenant (customer), thinking about the return on your money for working with that person.

I have seen negotiations that would make an investor over $20,000 break off over paint that would cost $500. You can do the math on that one.

This investor wasn't looking at this person as dollars. If he was, and he realized the dollars these people represented, he would have and should have spent the money to secure those dollars. The success of your investment in rental property hinges on these decisions.

In business or investing, each person or customer we come in contact with has a value to them. Our job is to determine the value, and if justified, establish the relationship needed to maximize it.

Investment in rental property is a business, and as with any other one, it is a heck of a lot easier to keep good existing customers (or tenants) than it is to find new ones that are good.

That is why I just spent $300 on a new BBQ for some good tenants that I have. I could have said no, it was not my obligation to do it. But through working with them over the last three years (remember, I am 'working' with them, investment in rental property is a business) I have realized they are people I want to continue dealing with.

It is because I see the dollars in our relationship and because I value them. And little things like a BBQ help them value me as well.

Oh and by the way, I didn't even flinch at the request, I smiled and agreed.

32
"Attention All Canadian Real Estate Websites, Blogs, Posts & Everyone Else - We Have News for You...Your House is NOT an Asset!"

There are tons of Canadian real estate websites and articles explaining why buying your own home is a person's best investment. They claim it's an asset.

Then you turn to the Baby Boom generation who support this claim with comments like, "Buying my own home was the best investment I ever made." Then, they make it even worse by saying, "Work hard to pay off your mortgage as fast as possible."

Sheesh, it's enough to drive you mad. It takes a pretty tough person to go against everything the media spreads on Canadian real estate websites as accepted truths.

I think that lately there's more and more of us who have enough financial education to understand that buying your own home is a great idea, but it's not the Holy Grail it was once made out to be.

And it's definitely not an asset from my point of view.

Whenever I get into this argument with people, they'll define asset in a million different ways. I think a little conversation around this is important.

Let me explain with a summary of conversations we get into over here pretty regularly.

I know several people who have a financial freedom plan of "paying off their mortgage". This idea is often even encouraged by the mainstream media on Canadian real estate websites as the primary path to wealth.

So they work hard every day to do just that -- making extra payments towards their mortgage, even.

Now, if your goal is to pay off your mortgage, then I don't think you're doing anything wrong here. You're on the right track.

BUT

If your goal is to achieve some sort of financial freedom with this plan, then you may be running down the wrong path.

Why?

Well, I've never, ever, ever met anyone who has become financially "free" by paying off their mortgage as a stand-alone strategy. And that's something that is not discussed on Canadian real estate websites.

Because once your mortgage is paid off, then what? If you want to live off the money in your house, can you?

No, you have to invest it somewhere. And to do that intelligently, you need some financial knowledge.

If the only thing you've been doing is paying off your mortgage and maybe buying the odd mutual fund unit in your self-directed RRSP, you probably can't take the equity in your house and turn it into cash flow.

Why not? Because you don't have the financial "know how" and experience to do it.

You've wasted 10,15,20,25 even 40 years paying off your mortgage, and now you're left with an "asset" that produces no income for you. And it's the only financial strategy you know, because we're really not taught much else in school, or by family, friends or on any Canadian real estate websites.

And this thing you are calling an "asset" actually costs you money.

You have to pay insurance on the house, you have utilities to pay and you have general maintenance (roof, furnace etc.).

And try not paying your property taxes. Your local government will be happy to take your "asset" off your hands if you don't cough up their money.

To us, an asset is something that pays for itself. Your house doesn't pay for itself.

Now, maybe you're reading this, but have an urge to scream:

"BUT HOLD ON GUYS, I'VE ALSO BEEN SAVING 10% OF MY INCOME!"

Well, now we're talking! But there's a catch here too.

What have you been doing with that 10%?

And please don't tell me you've been holding it in cash. Every time I read an article on Canadian real estate websites explaining that the government has pumped another billion dollars into the economy because of a "credit crunch", I cringe.

I do not have a PHD in economics, but if you are printing off new dollars and putting them into the market, what happens to the value of the dollars that were already in my pocket?

Hmmm. Well, I guess they go down in value, because there are now more dollars in circulation. Not good.

And with the value of my dollar decreasing, will things like food and oil go up in price? I'll bet they will (as they have been).

When I "retire", will my dollars be worth more or less than today? Probably less, much less. Hmmm.

These are strange times.

So if you're "saving" 10% of your income, I would ask your financial advisor for his/her thoughts on this stuff. And you can start ignoring most of what you read on Canadian real estate websites, too.

My personal philosophy is to be an "active investor". To purchase "assets" that pay for themselves and that you directly control. To teach yourself about money, investing, cash flow and taxes so that you can decide where to put your efforts.

Let's get back to how your house is not an asset.

If the value of your house has appreciated, and you're feeling pretty good about it, just remember: in order to directly benefit from that, you must learn how to take that stale equity inside your house and turn it into income.

Because even if you become totally "mortgage free", then what?

If you don't know how to turn the equity into income what exactly are you going to do with that equity?

Hand it over to a financial advisor for an annual 10% return?

10% is decent for the average Joe/Jill, but it's not going to pay for trips around the world with your family. It's likely not going to be enough for very much at all. You're going to need higher returns on your money to really have "financial freedom".

I think we need to change the discussion on Canadian real estate websites from "your home is a great investment" to "what are you doing to create income streams for yourself?"

And by focusing on answers to that second question, you'll move much faster towards the financial freedom you're looking for.

Now go do something about it and stop reading!

33
"Real Life Real Estate Investing May Require You to Get Upset - A Lot"

Real life real estate investing requires a certain order of priorities.

We'll explain by tackling one of the most common things we hear from people who "want to invest". They even know the importance of it. But when we ask why they don't, they respond with, **"I just don't have the time right now** to get into real life real estate investing."

We all live busy lives. Family, kids, friends, school, careers, both parents working, single parent working, older parents living with you. The list is endless.

However, I often wonder how much thought these people are putting into their answer.

If you've been hanging around us for a while, you've heard us say that the middle class thinks "month to month" and the wealthy think "year to year". Real life real estate investing requires a long term approach.

My fear is that these people are so caught up in the noise of their daily lives that they'll wake up a few short years from now, wondering how they ended up 10 years older with no real income producing assets to their name. Still trading time for money.

And my strong belief is that it boils down to priorities and values.

For example, a working Mom may have this list of values in this order:

1. Family
2. Community/Friends
3. Career

4. **Personal Time**
5. **Asset Accumulation**

And a working Dad may have a list that looks like this:

1. **Career**
2. **Family**
3. **Community/Friends**
4. **Personal Time**
5. **Asset Accumulation**

When you look at this list, it becomes blatantly obvious why someone wouldn't "have the time" to do some real life real estate investing.

They're so busy with their jobs and their family that it's tough to fit anything else in.

I can totally respect that. We've been taught that our "careers" are how we define ourselves and that job security actually exists. So it naturally ends up high on the value list.

Have you read this quote from Stephen Covey? It sums things up nicely:

"Most people spend their whole lives climbing the ladder of success only to realize, when they get to the top, the ladder has been leaning against the wrong wall."

Make sure your value list isn't leading you up the wrong wall.

You MUST take control of your own life. You must have personal responsibility.

You cannot depend on a company's RRSP plan. Just look at the equity markets these days. If you put all your eggs in someone else's basket, they ultimately have control.

You need to be the one that has control. And real life real estate investing is all about control.

Does that take more time and effort?

Yes.

Here's what happens next. One day, someone upsets them at their job and they finally lose it. They say to themselves that they must take control of their financial future.

They pull out a piece of paper and write out some goals.

I will buy 5 properties this year and make $25,000/month off my investments within 2 years.

I know all about this type of thinking. Been there. Done that.

But you know what?

When you put these goals out there on a piece of paper and carry them around in your pocket, they just kinda sit there.

You can only "think" about them for so long. "The Secret" only works if you actually put in some sweat equity.

The world rewards value creation. You need to go out and get started.

I've written down goals and got a high from just looking at how glorious they seemed on paper.

But nothing ever happened until I started working on them.

Here's how to get things done.

The next time someone or some thing upsets you at work, and I mean really makes you furious, use that energy to your advantage!

Maybe it's a Sales VP who tries to squeeze out yet another insane monthly sales quota increase or another unproductive meeting or some of your work being ignored.

Whatever it is that causes you to get frustrated may be the missing ingredient you need to get going!

There's opportunity in every adversity, right?

It's that frustration that is your only chance at having "asset accumulation" move high enough on your value list to force any action.

Use that emotional energy to reset your goals and to break out of your comfort zone.

Let me ask you something:

What if you just bought 2 properties this year?

Each of them earning a positive cash flow of $250/month.

Wouldn't that pay for your car?

And instead of your money sitting in a Mutual Fund that will *hopefully* earn 5% a year (before tax and inflation chop into that), you'll have your money controlling $500,000 worth of property.

The mortgages on that property will be paid off by someone else. So your $50,000 investment (money used for down payment) is now leveraged in two good homes in good areas.

The cash flow pays for your next car, the tax advantages allow you take more money home from your current income than you were before, and you are gaining equity in the properties every month.

And the most important part...

10 years from now, you will have even greater cash flow because the mortgages will be paid down. That's real life real estate investing.

You can use the higher cash flow for university payments for the kids, support for the aging parents, or support for yourself (think trips to Tuscany, Greece, or Hawaii!).

Do you see why you must make income producing asset accumulation a priority on your value list?

You must make the time. "Not having enough time" to take control of your own future is a lazy excuse. Get out in the real world and mix it up a little.

Let us leave you with two quotes to get your real life real estate investing kicked into gear...

"Do one thing every day that scares you."
-*Eleanor Roosevelt US diplomat & reformer (1884 - 1962)*

"It is not the critic who counts: not the man who points out how the strong man stumbles or where the doer of deeds could have done better. The credit belongs to the man who is actually in the arena, whose face is marred by dust and sweat and blood, who strives valiantly, who errs and comes up short again and again, because there is no effort without error or shortcoming, but who knows the great enthusiasms, the great devotions, who spends himself for a worthy cause; who, at the best, knows, in the end, the triumph of high achievement, and who, at the worst, if he fails, at least he fails while daring greatly, so that his place shall never be with those cold and timid souls who knew neither victory nor defeat."
-*Theodore Roosevelt April 10, 1899*

34
Canadian Real Estate Foreclosures & "The Hype"

The mere mention of Canadian real estate foreclosures is enough to get a beginner investor jumping out of their chair in excitement.

While there are foreclosures that may represent good deals, there are a few things you should know about them.

Let us explain.

Canadian real estate foreclosures have a process that is followed and that process differs province-by-province.

Here in Ontario, the "Power of Sale" process is used by Ontario lenders to provide a speedy means of disposing of real estate.

The property is usually listed on the Multiple Listing Service (MLS) with a real estate agent. And the list price is usually at "fair market value".

So here in Ontario, if you find Canadian real estate foreclosures listed as "power of sale", it doesn't necessarily mean it's automatically "a deal".

However, we have been involved in Power of Sale purchases where there is money to be made. For example, one property was purchased for $930,000 and sold several months later for $1,250,000.

You should note, that was done by a team with some serious Canadian real estate foreclosures experience and deep enough pockets to carry the property for some time if it didn't sell.

Right now in Canada (July 2008), there are a ton of "seminars" advertising to Canadians that there is huge money to be made in the U.S. by buying U.S. foreclosures.

And they're taking bus tours to go buy them.

Almost like a ride at Canada's Wonderland!

We get invited to these U.S. events and Canadian real estate foreclosures all the time.

And regularly turn them down.

Most people know us as investors, so they don't understand why we're usually not interested.

Some people even get upset that we're not all jazzed up about the opportunity.

Here's why these things don't interest us much.

The property is less important than the team of people involved in the transaction and post-transaction.

We buy properties with these criteria:

1. They produce positive cash flow (or can be made to produce positive cash flow).

2. The location is a fundamentally sound area to invest (population, job and transportation growth).

3. The property itself is sound.

4. Our team of experts works in the area, or has trusted partners in the area (lawyers, inspectors, contractors, mortgage brokers, real estate brokers, property managers).

Here's what most people miss when they look at foreclosures, especially U.S. foreclosures.

You ready for it?

They usually miss every one of the four points above.

Every one of them!

Amazing eh?

It seems to us that people who don't follow the points above are "speculating" more than "investing".

Usually, the person pitching U.S. or Canadian real estate foreclosures to us doesn't know any details about the property other than the address and that "it's a good deal".

No comparable sales, no economic data on the area, no team on trusted experts on the streets locally. Nothing.

Scary.

Just because a property is advertised as a "good deal", we prefer that we KNOW it's a good deal because one of out trusted team members is intimately familiar with the area.

The other day (literally yesterday), we were sitting in one of our lawyer's offices and overheard a conversation where someone had purchased a power of sale property.

And because the team of "experts" this person used was not familiar with the process, they didn't negotiate that the property be "tenant free" on closing.

Now this person had purchased a property and had to deal with a tenant living in it.

The proper termination of tenancy procedure had not been followed, and this tenant did not plan on leaving.

This was a problem for the purchaser, and he was starting to sound like a motivated seller.

A few days earlier, he thought he had found a motivated seller (the bank) and now because he bought without the right people in place, he had the potential of becoming one!

Amazing, eh?

So the next time someone wants you to buy a piece of real estate "because its a good deal" make sure you review the four points above.

Remember: don't focus on just "the price".

Will the property make you money? How?

Will you have to be there locally to accomplish that? If so, and the property is in the U.S., do you have a team of people on the streets there that you can trust?

How are the economic fundamentals of the area?

What about the property itself? Never buy something sight unseen.

If something sounds like a lot of hype...it is. Ask the tough questions.

Real estate is exciting, and in our opinion, it's one of the best investment vehicles available, if done properly!

35
"Toronto Rental Properties Won't Make You Rich - But The Process of Acquiring Them Will!"

We've been involved in well over 100 Toronto rental properties over the last couple of years. All cash flow positive, by the way! We've seen all types of investors.

And we've met all types of "wanna be" investors.

Here's an observation for you:

Many people want to be rich and believe that buying a piece of real estate will make them wealthy. They truly believe that Toronto rental properties are the key to wealth.

Now, in our humble opinion, real estate is a great vehicle to creating wealth. But it's not the real estate that makes you rich.

It's the stress, pressure, creative problem solving, emotional intelligence, people skills, communication skills, "never say die" attitude that makes you rich.

Let me share a story.

Situation #1

We were working with one individual who wanted to buy a piece of investment real estate and wanted us to take care of everything for him. And I mean everything.

Getting the tenants, negotiating positive cash flow, changing over the utilities, placing ads, dealing with lawyers, mortgage brokers, home inspectors, everything.

We've done it so many times now, that it's pretty easy for us.

He's never done it. He's looked at a lot of Toronto rental properties, but he's never really managed to get his hands dirty.

Well, we managed to get him a positive cash flow property.

Easy as pie.

Situation #2

We have been working with another member who has four investment properties. All purchased in the last 12 months. She is doing this all by herself.

She has negotiated the leases, she has dealt with home inspectors, she has handled mortgage problems as they popped up, she has dealt with several lawyers at closing, she has contacted contractors and she has evicted one tenant and put another one in the same house...earning her even more cash flow.

And during that process, she found another tenant, bought them a house and made another cash flow investment out of a bad situation.

Neat, eh?

Now let me ask you something...

If both of the above people lose all their real estate tomorrow because Martians land on earth and take all their Toronto rental properties away from them....who will build their wealth back faster?

Well the guy in situation #1 has the ability to call people. And that is a valuable skill. He should be commended for getting into real estate investing.

But we both know that the answer is obvious.

The lady in situation #2 will build back her wealth much faster.

She has the ability to handle anything. Nothing scares her any more. She knows opportunity comes out of adversity. She has experienced it herself. She has battled through. Her brain is now wired differently...she's not scared of very much, any more. Even Martians.

The process of investing in four real estate investments and handling issues as they popped up have made her a warrior.

We're not sharing this to convince you to buy real estate properties.

This lesson applies to anything. Not just buying Toronto Rental Properties.

The person who battles adversity to get through law school, or beats the odds to start their own business is also a warrior.

It's the process that makes people rich. It's experiencing the emotional roller coaster of any worthwhile achievement that makes you strong.

We've all read how lottery winners lose all their money a few short years after winning it.

Ever wonder why?

They haven't battled through the process of earning it.

Recently, I read about a lucky family who had a dream home built for them. They were part of the ABC TV show "Extreme Home Makeover".

The mayor of the city and thousands of volunteers even raised money to pay off their mortgage.

Guess what they did?

They took a $400,000 mortgage on the property and have been served with foreclosures papers because they have defaulted on the mortgage.

They didn't earn the money.

They didn't go through the process.

When you really decide that you are going to create wealth in your life, when you have 100% conviction about it, you will welcome the obstacles. You will welcome the things that others are fear.

Because that's what makes all the difference.

The process makes you rich. And not just in monetary terms.

To your success!

36
Rental Real Estate Investing – Some Financing Tips to Consider Before You Make Your Move

Rental real estate investing is riddled with hurdles and unanswered questions around financing.

When one bank denies your investment property mortgage request, another mysteriously approves you.

In Canada, there's an obvious need for better service in this area. As an investor in Canada, you are left to figure out rental real estate investing financing, mortgage insurance, property insurance and property taxes on your own.

It can be daunting, especially for you first time. And just when you don't think it can get any worse, try and find a bank or mortgage broker or financial planner that will help you lay down a 5-10 year plan that maps out how you can buy more than 4 or 5 investment properties in Canada.

Unless you are willing to put 20-25% down on each investment property, not many people have answers for you.

We've mapped out some information on investment property mortgages as a guide for you here.

Here are some additional Rental Real Estate Investing Tips

1. Hunt for a mortgage broker, banker of financial planner with actual real estate financing experience. Someone with experience will not only streamline the mortgage process, but they will also be able to give you some guidance.

For example, if you're looking to get a 5% down investment property mortgage, there are mortgage insurance fees that need to be accounted for in how you structure your investment. Some of these fees are high, and you don't want to be surprised by them on the day of closing.

And more importantly, some mortgage programs in Canada will allow you to "off set" other rental real estate mortgages if you have valid leases for them. This is a HUGE advantage in qualifying for more properties, because your debt ratio calculations don't suffer from previous rental real estate mortgages you've acquired.

2. It's always a good idea to look into the property tax rates in the area so you get an idea of how much you're going to pay. Most cities and towns will have them posted right on their website.

    You can also usually see the prior year's rates and get an idea of how fast they are trending up.

3. Try to develop a relationship with at least one bank and one mortgage broker. I don't believe most Canadians know this, but not all banks will have access to the best investment property mortgages and not all mortgage brokers will have access to all of the available mortgage products on the market.

    For example, banks at the national level will typically not deal with student rental properties, but at the "branch" level you may find them more willing to finance them.

    Both mortgage specialists directly from the bank and good mortgage brokers are extremely valuable to you.

    Once you find a good one, treat them with care.

    We've been saved many times by the sharp eye and experience of these contacts.

4. One day, a bank may have no decent real estate investment financing mortgages and the very next they may have a 10%

down open mortgage at the best interest rate possible. Make sure you are getting the latest information.

Real Estate investment financing products change almost monthly at every Canadian bank. Be on the look out.

5. Before you commit to your rental real estate investing financing, get in touch with your insurance company. I've seen insurance companies distance themselves from certain investment properties.

   If you don't have insurance on the property before closing, the real estate investment financing will fall apart. You don't want to be left scrambling for insurance the day before closing.

   Try to find an insurance agent who is aggressively building his business. Some agents that have are established don't want to deal with a "one off" rental property and will either brush you off or force you to switch ALL your properties to them. This is not necessary. If you are being forced to do this - keep looking!

6. This next tip really isn't about the real estate investment financing itself. It's more about the source of the advice you're getting.

   After a mortgage broker or real estate professional knows that you're excited about rental real estate investing, you may find them emailing you little flyers outlining the details of what they believe is a good real estate investment. And because it's coming from a professional, you may be tempted to believe their opinion.

   When these deals cross our desks, we're often shocked. The prices are too high, the rents are unrealistic and the exit plan doesn't exist. Take advice from actual investors only.

7. If part of your investing plan involves possibly selling the property before the term of the mortgage is up, make sure you

check out the penalties you'll have to pay to break the mortgage early.

It'll usually be about 3 months' interest and you'll want to factor that into your numbers. Some real estate investment financing will waive most of the penalty if you move the mortgage from one property to another within a certain time frame.

And there you have it. Some of our rental real estate investing financing favorites.

37
"Real Estate Investing Opportunities Can Create Lifetime Value for You"

Checking out real estate investing opportunities can be exhausting.

So recently, we've been reading *The Last Lecture* by Randy Pausch and it has stirred a lot of reflection. If you haven't heard about the book, it's the last message of a man dying from cancer leaves for his family. He passed away this past July.

It's a fantastic book and a heart warming story.

And it really got us thinking.

I have a six your old son and a two year old daughter. After reading this book, I started formalizing some messages that I would want to make sure were passed along to them.

Now listen up! I'm not dying and I plan on being here for a very long time, so don't get the wrong idea! But what this book did was make me formalize some messages around all areas of my life, not just real estate investing opportunities.

Some of them are very private and I may share them down the road, however, because we're here to talk about real estate investing opportunities, I want to share one of the messages with you because it directly applies to this theme.

It's this:

You will have much more freedom in your life if you always work for "Future Value" instead of "Now Value".

Let me explain with a story.

A very good friend of mine (who is accumulating some very big wealth in his life) was commenting on how confused he after speaking with a Senior Vice President in a software company. He was making an exceptionally high salary, but had no freedom and was living "paycheck to paycheck".

This friend of mine started from nothing six years ago, and is now on track to have millions of dollars in equity and cash flow in his life.

He doesn't have a higher education. He doesn't have all the "right" connections. And he didn't have a helping hand in creating his wealth.

But he did have a strong work ethic. Very strong.

And he is able to magically handle any problem that is thrown his way. Literally, anything. Nothing is a problem for him. He just continues moving forward. It's jaw dropping and inspiring.

So he was confused by this VP, because growing up, he figured if you were a Vice President of a company, you wouldn't be living paycheck to paycheck. And you would have a big mansion with gates and stuff!

He had always assumed that people with advanced degrees and big job titles had it made. And because he didn't have a fancy degree or hang out in the right social circles, he worked terribly hard.

And now, over the next 24 months, his income and wealth is set to explode. Massively.

And do you know why?

Most people work on things that have a "now value". He always worked on things that had a "future value".

This is the biggest lesson I want to pass on to my children.

So what do I mean by this?

When you are working at your job, everything you do has a now value. You work and you get paid. There's no future benefit for you. None.

Even if you are in sales at a big software company, and work 2 years to "land that big account" and earn a mega commission cheque -- it's still just "now value". There's no recurring revenue.

You've spent two years of your life to create income at one point in time. If that big account comes back to buy more stuff in a few years, the commission or benefit of this will go to the company. You may be long gone.

But if you work to create future value, then the benefits begin to multiply.

For example, if you work to create your own business, you create cash flow and create equity in the business for yourself. You are creating "now value" and "future value".

Now, starting your own business has its risks of course, so let's look at what my friend did and still does.

For the last six years, he has been working on his real estate portfolio and taking advantage of real estate investing opportunities. He was buying houses, working on those houses and then selling them for a profit. He was also buying houses and getting tenants to rent the houses from him.

He was creating "future value". And he didn't even know it.

Because when you start out, everything seems difficult. The light at the end of the tunnel seems so far away. It's hard to see the "big picture". But because the type of work he chose to focus on naturally has a future value built into it, he was set to benefit massively from his efforts.

Now all the work he has been doing over the last six years is coming back to him in multiples.

The equity in his real estate portfolio has grown dramatically (we're talking big dollars) AND he has positive cash flow from his real estate investing opportunities.

So he worked once and he is getting paid multiple times.

With some of the real estate investing opportunities, he generated income by selling properties, he gets appreciation from the real estate he has kept, he gets cash flow from his rental properties, he gets tax advantages that allow him to pay less in taxes and his equity in the real estate continues to build and compound.

And after accumulating a bunch of real estate, things start taking off.

For example, if you went out and picked up 4 small income properties for a grand total of $1,000,000 and then the market goes up 5%, your net worth goes up $50,000. You didn't work any harder for that. Your asset base of real estate delivered it to you.

And if the market goes up the next year, your net worth goes up again. You didn't have to do anything else. You worked to acquire the properties once and you are reaping the future rewards. And the whole time, the properties are producing positive cash flow for you.

This doesn't all happen in a straight line. The market moves sideways sometimes, but if you are getting positive cash flow from your properties, it's no big deal.

Positive cash flow properties are easy to hang on to.

Even in bad economic times, positive cash flow real estate pays for itself. It's like a mini, little business working away for you. That's why we like real estate investing opportunities so much.

Back to this VP...

I mean no disrespect to him. None at all.

I'm just pointing out that when you focus all the productive hours of your day on work that pays you only once, you are not leveraging yourself. That VP can easily continue doing what he does and start working on some "future value" on the side. Perhaps a little side business, or some cash flow real estate.

When you focus on putting your efforts on work that has "future value", the benefits multiply. You earn income today and you will earn income again from the same work in the future as a bonus. You don't actually have to put in much effort to gain the future value.

If you are reading these articles, then you're in the middle of some of our own "future value" work.

This article can be used again and again. We're creating this once and it will be used many times.

And the email list that we are working to create today will have years of value to us. There is immediate value in this newsletter and there is future value, because we get to use it again and again.

Focus on future value in everything you do.

"Now Value" is a quick fix. But like everything that is a quick fix, it's likely not worth it in the long run.

So the message to my children is this:

Do what makes you excited. Life is obviously too short for anything else.

And to really leverage your efforts, to really create some personal freedom, build in some "future value" to the work you do.

To your success!

38
Your Real Estate Investment Business Plan

We were recently asked to answer some high level real estate investment business plan questions for a national Canadian magazine. They were putting a piece together for someone looking to get started with real estate investing.

Through the magic of editing, the article ended up carrying only a small portion of our answers ... so ... here are the unedited answers to the original questions in all their glory ;) The nice image in the corner is by theplerolsen

Enjoy!

1. What are some things to consider when starting out?

Real estate investing is a business, so naturally, you need a real estate investment business plan. Spend some time deciding how much capital you have to begin with and how much time you are willing to invest. These decisions made early will help you decide what types of transactions you want to get involved with.

Also, it's important to read and acquire good real estate information, but there's no need to spend years buried in theory. Find an experienced mentor, surround yourself with an experienced team of professionals and then get started. Ultimately, the people around you will increase the chance of success of your real estate investment business plan. Many beginner investors don't realize this critical point and focus on the "the deal" instead of the people. A solid real estate investment business plan is more important to you than finding one good deal. Good deals are everywhere, a solid real estate investment business plan will keep you going in the right direction.

2. How is buying your first investment property different from buying a primary residence?

When you buy an investment property, there will be several differences. However, with residential real estate investing (properties with four units or less) the differences are mostly minor.

The primary ones to be aware of are mortgage insurance and property insurance.

If you put less than 20% down on a residential investment property, there is mortgage insurance just like a primary residence, however, the rates for investment properties are typically much higher. You will want to be aware of these fees when working out the carrying costs of the property. Also, the property insurance you will need is slightly different. You will want rental property insurance. If you have tenants in the property, then you may want to request that they obtain contents insurance. That way, you have insured the property yourself and the tenants have insured their belongings inside.

If you buy an investment property with 5 or more units, you'll be dealing with commercial mortgages. These mortgages have extra fees associated with them. The most common are mortgage broker fees that are charged with commercial mortgages and commercial property appraisal fees. You'll want take this into consideration in your real estate investment business plan.

And if you're buying a property to tear it down completely and rebuild the home, then you will likely require a construction loan. This type of loan product allows you to draw more money from the lender at predetermined stages of completion. You'll want to get a complete understanding of when you will have access to the funds, so that you can plan accordingly. With this, make sure you have your real estate investment plan reviewed by your banker, so that you are on the same page and financing hiccups don't kill your build. You don't want to become a motivated seller with a half built property.

3. What are some tips on negotiating?

Timing, information and strategy are keys to negotiating an investment property. Any long term real estate investment business plan should include continued education in sales and negotiation. A small 3% savings on a $300,000 property is $9,000 in your pocket.

Unlike a primary residence, you will likely have much more flexibility with your closing date when buying an investment property. Use that to your advantage. You may want to offer a quick closing instead of offering the seller's asking price. You would be amazed at how quickly you can negotiate a favourable price by using the closing date to your advantage.

Also, with the use of public records, you can find out when the property was purchased and for how much. If the property was purchased within the last year or two for a substantially lower price, perhaps there is more flexibility on the amount you purchase the property for. Or, if the seller has moved into another home, perhaps they are making multiple mortgage payments and are motivated to sell. When you find out any information on the Seller's situation, ask yourself how you can use that to your advantage.

And lastly, if you are ever verbally negotiating a price, try not to be the one who names a number first. Let the Seller speak first. If you answer first, you could be paying a lot more for the property than required. Perhaps the Seller was willing to accept much less than your first offer. If you are asked how much you would offer on a property answer with a question. For example, "If I was able to close on the property quickly what would be the best you could do?"

4. What are some short term and long term goals to keep in mind with your real estate investment business plan?

Initially, you will want to focus on cash flow. Calculate how much positive cash flow the property will produce every month.

No matter how you do the math, if the property costs you money to carry, then it likely isn't a very good investment. Many beginners convince themselves that a negative cash flow property is a good investment, because the appreciation of the property will more than make up for the monthly losses. That strategy backfires more often than it succeeds. Ask anyone who purchased at the top of a market cycle. Appreciation of a property can never be guaranteed. Be suspicious of anyone who tells you otherwise.

Long term, you will want to focus on how large of a real estate asset base you would like to own. Positive cash flow real estate will produce monthly income and pay down the mortgage. Over time, you'll own the asset free and clear. At that point, the positive cash flow will be much higher and your net worth will have increased substantially. You can then refinance and pull out substantial amounts of capital, or use the cash flow for other investments. And if you do pull out some equity on a rental property, your tenants will help pay the mortgage down again. This is what makes real estate such a beautiful thing!

So, in your real estate investment business plan, decide initially on a cash flow amount you would like to achieve on each property to make it a good investment. Then, decide how much real estate you will need to own "free and clear" to produce the income you desire.

5. Is it more profitable to manage a property on your own, or hire a property manager?

If it's a single family home or anything up to a four unit property, it will be much more profitable to manage it on your own. Good property managers do exist, but can be tough to find. Property maintenance and unexpected repairs can eat up cash flow at an alarming rate, especially when you pay a premium via a property manager to handle these expenses.

If it's a larger commercial property (5 or more units), you may find it too time consuming to manage yourself and a property manager will be a requirement. A vacancy rate and property management fees should be included in your real estate investment business plan when working out the carrying costs of these properties.

Also, as a beginner, it's very important to understand how to manage a property successfully yourself. The experience you gain managing a small residential investment property will be invaluable to you when you do eventually hire a property manager because you will have an intimate understanding of how the property should be run.

6. In your opinion, what is the most sound type of real estate investment (ex. Flip, buy-hold-rent, etc.)?

A positive cash flow buy-hold-rent property is by far a superior investment. Although "flipping" homes sounds fun and looks sexy on TV, it is more like speculating than investing. When you flip a property, you try to buy it for one price, hoping that someone else buys it from you for a higher price in the future.

Even if you put some great improvements into the property, you'll have mortgage payments and renovation costs during the time you hold it. If the market changes during this time, you could be left holding the property much longer than anticipated. Each month that you hold the property with money going out to cover carrying costs and no money coming in, you will gradually turn into the classic "motivated seller" other buyers are looking to take advantage of.

Also, when flipping properties, you usually have to deal with contractors and suppliers. You can end up turning yourself into a project manager instead of an investor. It can be more like creating a new job for yourself than anything else. Calculate how many hours you will spend on flipping the property and then divide it by the expected profit after taxes, real estate fees, legal fees, mortgage payments, insurance, mortgage payments, property taxes and insurance. If the number comes out lower than expected, don't be surprised. You wouldn't be the first person who figured they could have made more money with less stress flipping burgers instead of flipping homes!

A sophisticated real estate investment business plan is looking to build an asset base of cash flow properties. They invest their money and look for a good return on their money quickly. They are generally not "flippers".

True investors look to buy and control assets. Look at Warren Buffet. He buys enough shares to control a company. He then uses the cash flow of the company to make other investments. A buy-hold-rent strategy is very similar. You are buying the property to control the asset and then direct the cash flow to your own benefit.

If you do decide to flip, you must purchase well below market value. You will likely go over any budget you set. Check your numbers and then have a mentor review them.

7. What are your top 5 real estate investing tips?

i. Your real estate investment business plan should always focus on real estate in fundamentally good communities. Look for population growth, higher than average family incomes and expanding transportation routes. These communities hold their value well and will often appreciate strongly.

ii. After you've found a good community, then find a solid property. An attractive home will always rent easier and sell faster. You protect yourself by purchasing a good property in a good community. And starter homes will typically not rise and fall as fast and hard as high end luxury real estate.

iii. Don't buy a property because it's a "good deal". Buy a property because it is in demand and will sell or rent quickly.

iv. Your real estate investment business plan should involve surrounding yourself with an experienced team. The team is more important than the property because they will steer you around obstacles that you may not even be aware of. Look for real estate brokers, mortgage brokers, lawyers and accountants with real estate *investing* experience and not just real estate experience.

v. Most people create a real estate investment business plan that will over estimate what they can accomplish in one year and underestimate what they can accomplish in ten. Keep the big picture in mind and never stop driving towards it! Keep things in perspective and expect bumps along the way, ultimately they make you stronger.

39
A Real Estate Investing Club Is Only As Good As the People In It

There's something not often discussed at the local real estate investing club meetings.

Real estate can be a tough business, very tough.

Navigating the sea of lawyers, home inspectors, mortgage brokers, real estate sales reps, accountants, contractors, insurance companies and real estate investing club meetings can be daunting.

But you must never give up. Ever.

Building a team of professionals around you who know what they are doing is by far the single most important thing you can be doing. They are the most important piece and should be considered your main partners in your real estate investing club.

It's so much more important than the actual investment property. If you're just starting out, creating an asset base of real estate for yourself you may be so focused on the property or attending the latest real estate investing club meeting that you lose sight of the big picture.

Well we're here to make sure that doesn't happen.

You see, investment properties have been around a long time. And they'll continue to be around for a long time. Shelter is "a need", after all. It's one of the nice things about investing in real estate -- people actually need it.

However, many investors get so caught up in finding "a deal" that they burn a lot of bridges along the way.

We've seen many a "real estate investing club" miss this important detail.

Here's a quick list of the most common team building mistakes we've seen missed in local real estate investing club discussions:

1. Working with a lawyer for a few days, only to discover that you can save $50 by using a different lawyer. Pulling all the property closing files from lawyer #1 and sending them to lawyer #2. What you didn't know was the advice lawyer #1 gives you on closing day could save you thousands of dollars. Will lawyer #1 take you back as a client when you really need his advice? Maybe, but I've seen many people crawl back to a good lawyer only to be turned away.

2. Using two mortgage brokers at the same time to try and save a tenth of a percent off your mortgage rate. Because you didn't tell them about each other, they are both working hard for you....even making commitments on your behalf with underwriters. At the last minute you pull the plug broker #1 and go with #2. A few weeks later, you want to buy another property and the broker you burned bridges with has private money ready to make it happen but decides he will never work with you again. You end up going to another broker and paying much more in fees than you needed to!

3. An accountant charges a fee of $500 to share some tactics around structuring your real estate. Following the advice will save you thousands of dollars in taxes and prevent costly litigation. You decide to take his/her advice and run. You don't pay the bill because you'll just tell your own accountant to implement your new found knowledge and he'll do it for free. When it's done incorrectly, you end up facing a huge tax bill.

4. A real estate sales rep shows you 6 multiplexes that fit your criteria. She spends days previewing the properties and focuses on areas that she knows are fundamentally strong investment areas. You decide to try and save some cash and negotiate directly with the listing sales rep to save some commission. You call your agent back when you're ready to buy another property and your calls go unanswered. You spend precious time trying to find someone else with the same caliber of knowledge and experience.

5. You have an insurance agent quote you on 5 investment properties. Another insurance company gives you a better price. Instead of giving the first insurance contact an opportunity to match the price or explain differences, you pull the plug and go with the cheaper company.

In the short term each of these moves may seem like the prudent thing to do. After all if you can save $50 or shave off $100 from your annual insurance bill, why not, right?

Here's the thing...

You end up burning a lot of bridges along the way. And when you are just starting out, you may not realize how small of a world it really is. Mortgage brokers talk to each other, so do lawyers, accountants and real estate sales reps. When you're really in a jam one day and need an experienced real estate lawyer, he/she may no longer be willing to work with you.

That $50 you saved up front may end up costing you thousands. Seriously, we've seen it with our very own eyes.

The most valuable thing you are building is your team, not your properties. Even if you are thinking about taking your business elsewhere, because you have every right to do that, make a quick phone call explaining your decision. It *may* save the relationship.

Let me take an extreme example to explain this further.

When Trump ran into serious problems in the early 1990s with his real estate, he was able to rebuild.

Why?

Although he was a tough negotiator, he always treated the people around him very well. He had his own all star team.

Using that team, he was able to re-assemble his empire.

Sure, he had some experience at that point. But he also had his team. He had people like George Ross by his side.

He didn't have George when he was just starting out. George is part of his team.

When your property springs a leak, or the financing gets difficult, or you need a contractor ASAP....it's your team that will help you out.

Have you noticed how Robert Kiyosaki, the author of *Rich Dad Poor Dad*, constantly talks about investment real estate? You may not have noticed that he doesn't work alone. He has a team of property managers that go in and handle his apartment buildings for him. They are the ones who fix up the building and raise the rent (improving the cash flow and the value).

All wealthy investors work the same way.

We were just speaking with the top apartment consultant in Canada. He's the kind of guy that saves you from costly investment mistakes. Definitely someone you want on your team for the long haul.

The most valuable asset in your portfolio is not the properties.

It's your team. They are your *primary* real estate investing club.

Build it, nurture it, take care of it and it will pay off with large returns.

40
Real Estate Investing Courses Have Some Critical Numbers You Should Focus On...

Some of the best real estate investing courses have always covered these important topics:

Net Operating Income

Net Operating Income is commonly used to analyze real estate investments and it's really very straightforward.

Net Operating Income = Gross Operating Revenue (minus vacancy and collection losses) - Operating Expenses (excluding debt service and taxes)

Now, a few accountants in the room may start tweaking this a little bit to include depreciation and/or Non-Operating income, but for most purposes, the above formula is accepted as standard. This is the way it's covered in many real estate investing courses.

So, in residential real estate investments, you determine a property's Net Operating Income by taking the Revenue and subtracting the Expenses.

Revenue will typically be generated by the rent on the property and perhaps any other income (like renting out parking spaces separately or having coin operating laundry machines on site).

And expenses will be things like advertising, insurance, property taxes, maintenance, any property management and utilities (if you are paying for them instead of the tenant).

So, if you have a home you are renting out for $1,650/month and your tenant is paying the utilities, your monthly expenses may include things like insurance and property taxes. Let's say that comes to $275/month.

So your annual Net Operating Income would be:

Operating Income.........................$1650 x 12
Operating Expenses......................- $275 x 12
Net Operating Income....................= $16,500/year

Different real estate investing courses will have you fine tune these numbers with vacancy ratios and other minor expenses, but the above gives you a quick example of Net Operating Income.

An important note: your debt service (or mortgage payments) is not included in Net Operating Income calculations.

Capitalization Rates

Capitalization Rates are used quite often in larger real estate investments. It's an attempt to look at how fast the property will pay for itself. We've spent entire days in real estate investing courses on this topic alone.

In North America, the most often used formula for this is:

Net Operating Income / Cost or Value of the Property = Capitalization Rate

Many first time investors search out for properties that have a capitalization rate of 10% or higher. In most large cities, the reality is that for larger investment properties (like apartment buildings), it's difficult to find anything above 7%.

There is currently a lot of demand for such properties and investors are willing to take 7% or even lower capitalization rates on these.

Here's an example. If a property produces $50,000 in Net Operating Income (or positive cash flow) and the cost of the property was $500,000..

$50,000 / $500,000 = .1 or 10% Capitalization Rate

The property will pay for itself in 10 years.

41
Real Estate Investing Education: You Need To Get Good At "Macro" and "Micro"

When I first decided to "get rich" with my real estate investing education, I had grand plans (and still do).

I was really good at reading all sorts of books about visualization and affirmations, and I would "see" myself flying around in helicopters visiting all of my properties all around the world.

For the record, our properties are all in Canada unless you count my family's land in Croatia, but that's part family vineyards, part farm, part old style European village, part "in the middle of nowhere". Our father never hesitates to remind us that it has real value, because it's 20 minutes from the Adriatic coast, and who knows, he could be right.

Anyhoo...back on point...

So I would visualize and come up with big plans and write out big goals and repeat them everyday. And I actually still believe in that stuff.

But by the time I turned 30, I had this realization that unless I start focusing on the little things, the big things would never happen. My real estate investing education alone wasn't enough.

Have you ever heard a person say, "I'm a big picture guy/gal, don't bother me with the details - I'm not good at that stuff".

Well, that was me.

Always focused on the big picture.

And always ignoring the little details.

My personality really thrives on big ideas and I'm an Aquarius, so I've always been told I'm a "dreamer", so I guess I just ran with it.

But over time, I started to notice that almost everyone who told me they were good at the "big vision" stuff and "not-so-great with the details stuff" was dead broke or close to it. But they all seemed to have a lot of real estate investing education.

About the same time, I noticed that the millionaire-makers devoted themselves to being good at both. They may not get obsessed with the details of balance sheets, but they have a understanding of them.

They balanced the importance of bottom line results with progressive thinking.

I'm constantly reminded of these days. Since starting our own business, Nick and I have constantly been forced to watch the bottom line and "think big" simultaneously. It's been a "new" type of real estate investing education.

And thankfully, he's better at the details than I am. We're a good match and the chemistry is just right.

One of us without the other couldn't have pulled off what we've started, but together we're unstoppable.

There's a lot of chatter right now about "outsourcing" and using "virtual assistants" for the things you're not good at. And we're big believers in that.

But don't confuse outsourcing website design with outsourcing your bookkeeping. You may not need to be the person entering all your receipts into MS Excel or QuickBooks, but you better be the person watching the cash flow coming and going.

You'd better be the person raising funds for your business.

You'd better be the person taking 100% responsibility for sales in your business.

You'd better be the person stepping up and filling a vacant property.

You'd better be the person double checking the cash flow numbers.

You'd better be the person negotiating prices with contractors.

You'd better be the person looking over the details of your leases.

You'd better be the person in the trenches doing the real work day-in-day-out.

You'd better be the person understanding what your accountant is telling you.

You'd better be the person attending to the details of your empire.

Now, if you're a big picture person, don't get discouraged. There's a place for you.

Our real estate brokerage is partly the result of some "big picture" brainstorming on a yellow piece of "dollar store" Bristol board. Big visions and big dreams are necessary. And real estate investing education forms the base of your decision making.

But to realize your dreams, you'll need to focus on the "macro" *and* the "micro".

After you've built you're empire, whatever size that is for you, then you can outsource and hire people to handle the daily dirty work. But to get it all running, it's gotta be done by you.

Too many people miss that point or realize it too late and end up wasting a lot of time. Months, years, even decades can slip by quickly.

Time is one resource that we can't get back.

So keep dreaming but get to work ;) Until next time ... be a Renegade!

42
Real Estate Investment in Canada the Power of "Set It & Forget It"

It's amazing how quickly we forget things. Even though we discuss real estate investment in Canada around here almost every single day, we still manage to forget some of the powerful "basics".

What do I mean?

Let me explain.

When we started investing, we focused almost exclusively on the monthly cash flow a property generated.

So, for a typical real estate investment in Canada, if the mortgage + the property taxes + the insurance cost us $1,700, and we rented out the property for $1,900, then we had $200 in cash flow.

And even though each month, the mortgage was being paid down and every year, a little appreciation would occur, we basically ignored that stuff.

Not intentionally, it just happened. We couldn't touch and feel the mortgage reduction on a regular basis (we just got an annual statement and those are often quickly filed away), and appreciation just slowly sort of happens with little irregular spurts.

We have one real estate investment in Canada that we sort of "wrote off" for a little while, because we had to refinance it about 5 years ago to pull out equity for some renovations. So in our minds, I think we felt there wasn't much equity left in the property. And that feeling just kinda stuck.

On top of that, we had a feeling since day one on that property that we kinda overpaid for it by about 5%.

So, we really felt it would be a very long time before there was any sort of value in the property other than the monthly cash flow.

Well, it was a pleasant surprise this week when we found out that comparables for this real estate investment in Canada were selling for $70,000 more than we purchased our property for.

AND

Over the past five years, the mortgage has been paid down about $25,000.

So we know have approximately $80,000 of equity in the property. We don't have the full $95,000 ($70,000 + $25,000) because of the refinance mentioned earlier.

Needless to say, we're pretty happy about it.

The property is cash flowing nicely and has been for years, plus, now we have a chunk of equity in it.

This realization reminded me that the reason real estate is so great is because of the "set it and forget it" factor.

Once you have a real estate investment in Canada with tenants in it, you can get your hands on the monthly cash flow but you can't regularly touch the mortgage reduction or the appreciation.

You're forced into long term investing.

It's great.

In the past, with other investments I've had in the stock market, it's been easy for me to get at profits. And that's always made it tempting to withdraw and spend them. And I'm definitely guilty of that!

With real estate, after you accumulate a little portfolio of properties, the power of the "set it and forget" approach really begins to snowball.

For example, let's say you have 4 properties worth $250,000 each.

Each one cash flows at $200 per month.

You have $800 per month in profits to play with.

But after 5 years, if the market appreciates at only 2% a year, you've picked up $104,080 in equity on those properties. And if your mortgage was being reduced by $4,000 a year, then you've gained another $20,000 on each for a total of $184,080 in gains.

And you didn't really do anything "extra" yourself to gain that.

If the market continued gaining 2% for another 5 years, you've gained a total of $218,994 in equity in that property. And the mortgage would have been paid down another $20,000 on each (I'm being conservative here), for a total mortgage reduction of $160,000. That would mean you have a total of $378,994 in equity.

Don't forget about the cash flow you've been earning over those years, too.

Nice eh?

And 2% a year isn't really a stretch. Mild inflation would carry most properties along at that rate.

If you're a bit more daring and believe you may get an annual average of 5% appreciation on your 4 properties over 10 years, then you're looking at $628,894 in equity gains, plus the mortgage reduction of $160,000 for a total gain of $788,894.

And if you put 10% on those properties that would mean you invested $100,000 and got back $788,894 over 10 years.

Not bad at all.

Imagine you had 8 properties instead of 4? The numbers get big fast.

And none of this is including the cash flow from the properties.

Anyway, if you're reading this, I'm likely preaching to the converted here.

But we can all use a reminder a little once in a while.

Especially when you often only have the "negative" to focus on. Like cleaning carpets after one tenant moves out and spending your Saturday mornings trying to fill a property with someone else.

It can all seem futile, but treat this as a friendly little reminder that there are big pay days ahead of you for any real estate investment in Canada that you may have.

Slow and steady often wins the race.

And all of this reminds me of a mortgage broker, 5 years ago, swearing up and down about building wealth faster using "condo conversions" instead of rental properties.

Rentals were "too slow" for her.

Well, this week, the same week that we're realizing we have unexpected equity in one of our properties, I get a phone call.

It was an investor looking for some advice.

When the market was roaring forward a few years back, the condo conversion business was roaring, too.

But this investor on the phone now had $100,000 tied up in a condo conversion that they are having serious problems getting back because of slowing appreciation and project mismanagement. That $100,000 represented some profits from previous projects, and their initial capital investment.

It looks like they are running the risk of losing their entire real estate investment in Canada.

I'm not saying we've never made bad investments. We have.

It's just interesting that almost every single time someone pitches us with "easy/quick/fast money" investing, a story like this pops up sooner or later.

We're all guilty of going after "easy money". We have in the past. Who hasn't?

But, yet again, this week we were reminded of the power of steady, proven growth as the best approach for any real estate investment in Canada. And hopefully, this reminder keeps us (and you) on the straight and narrow.

You need these "slow and steady" growth reminders pounded over your head sometimes, don't you? It's so easy to get off track.

Ron Papiel, the kitchen gadget infomercial king, had a great catch phrase for his Ronco Rotisserie that applies directly to real estate investing...

"Set it and Forget it!"

We think he was bang on.

43
Mr. B & the Status Quo

We make a conscious effort to study the most prolific investors we see. One of the most impressive traits the biggest action takers possess is an aversion to the status quo.

I recall working in one of my first jobs out of University. It was a technical support call center position for Oracle Corporation.

We were the last line of defense for companies like the Royal Bank of Canada and other big companies who depended on the Oracle database for processing massive amounts of data every day.

If the database crashed, we were the firefighters who came in to save the day. It was stressful sometimes and a real pressure cooker. But I learned a lot - fast.

I recall when the rumblings began that our support department was going to be shut down and replaced by a support center in India.

This was back in 1999.

And for the next twelve months, all most people did was sit around and complain about it. They were happy to come in to work every day, miserable knowing that at any moment, they may get word that they were going to be out of work.

But I remember one guy in the office who stood out. Let's call him Mr. B. He didn't care about the rumours. Mr. B was planning out his next move even before the "India rumours" had begun.

When I asked about his plans, it became obvious that he came to Oracle for a set amount of time, for a specific purpose, and was planning his next move.

He was writing his database certification exams, maintaining a high work ethic at his current role and scoping out prospective employers for his next role.

He came in looking to get some high-end database skills and then was planning to be a database administrator for a pharmaceutical company. After that, he wanted to start his own consultancy.

During this time, I couldn't help notice that he was putting himself under some real pressure, but I assume he thought it was necessary to achieve his goals.

And several months later, he landed his big Database Administrator job, got a huge pay increase and was on his merry way.

He was the needle in the haystack. 98% of everyone else just sat around, waiting for their fate to be delivered to them.

How does this relate to real estate?

The most active investors we've seen come from all walks of life. Some are teachers, some are high-end super executives, some are young couples just getting started together, and some are parents planning for their children.

And most of them never rest. They are always on the go.

They are always working, moving forward, and improving themselves and their place in life.

It would be very easy for them to sit back and "punch the clock" every day. Who could really blame them? Most of the investors we meet are doing pretty well for themselves. But instead, they choose to create more for themselves.

They aren't satisfied. There's a certain hunger in them.

They have a plan and may not know exactly all the steps in that plan, but are willing to get started.

Knowing that the next step will magically appear when the first one is taken.

They are busy creating their own reality.

They are like Mr. B.

The vast majority your peers are extremely committed to keeping everything the same. Same job, same routine, same life. I'm not so certain that this is possible anymore. There was a time for that strategy, but that day has come and gone.

What exists as a stable job today can be gone tomorrow. Literally.

The vast majority of action-oriented investors we meet are working vigorously at their current role and simultaneously planning for and implementing a series of events and investments that will take care of them down the road.

It's a pressure cooker, but they seem to be able to handle it.

Just like Mr. B. It's amazing to watch.

And I would assume that if you're ready for this, you have a Mr. or Ms. B inside of you.

We're here to tell you that it's your aversion to accepting the "status-quo" in your life that will move you forward. It's the same trait that all successful action takers we've seen possess.

So if you find yourself juggling your current role, implementing actions for your next and planning for steps after that - then you've got what it takes to achieve whatever it is that you choose.

You have the same traits that we see in all massive action takers. Be proud.

Remember - Your Life. Your Terms.

Until next time ... be a Renegade!

44
Real Estate Investing Programs with "Two Monks Lost in Communist Corporate Canada"

Many of you know that as we researched real estate investing programs, we were both "stuck" in corporate Canada to varying degrees.

During that time, we started to build our real estate portfolios and then our real estate brokerage.

Literally for years, I would walk around like I was sleep-walking as I strolled through rows of blue/grey cubicle walls.

Although we had always spoken of wonderful ideas for new businesses, we felt trapped in our 9-5 ruts.

And it was so difficult to break out of it, because the pay was so good.

Golden handcuffs, if you will.

It was a "guilty pleasure" to consider changing course and doing what I really wanted to do. I always told myself that I had "responsibilities" to produce for my family.

Reflecting back on it all, somehow I think I got lost.

I'm not sure where, but I took a major wrong turn somewhere.

As a young adult in University, I had these big dreams of helping people, changing the world, making a difference!

And now, I was making good money, but it was spent on leather shoes, dress shirts and watches used as some sort of "corporate armour".

Many people reading this may hate what I'm going to say next but it holds true for me...

I felt like I was living in a communist country while working in Corporate Canada.

You really couldn't challenge the boss. You really couldn't put out your own creative corporate messages without getting press releases screened and approved "from above". And you had to "conform" to be just like every other corporate citizen in the organization, or risk a trip to Human Resources for some sort of assessment.

The only saving grace was that I got to leave and go home at night. I could dive into my real estate investing programs that I purchased off some teleseminar. They gave me some sort of escape.

Please don't misunderstand me. Corporate Canada has given me a lot. It taught me about discipline, routine and good habits. It taught me about responsibility and the importance of systems. And some of the leaders within the organizations I worked in will remain lifelong friends.

It just seemed for me that the structure of the corporate organization that had served me well for some years would never allow me to continue growing throughout my lifetime.

And the expressions on the faces of older executives seemed to confirm my suspicions.

Everyone seemed pissed off and stressed out.

Maybe that realization was a hidden driver behind our real estate investing and our real estate investing programs - I'm not sure.

But the real estate investing programs we invested in were one of the few "money making ideas" which we actually acted upon that would "get us out of here".

Real estate is not the only idea, of course. There are a million business models that may be better suited for you. And to be fair, some real estate investing programs are weighted too heavily on the "get-rich-quick" angle. Too much fluff in there.

In the book *Vagabonding* by Rolf Potts, there's a story of two monks who have made vows to never leave their monastery but keep telling each other that one day they will go out and see the world.

Knowing full well that they couldn't leave, they kept putting off their plans until "next summer" and then "to the next summer". Never actually accomplishing their goals.

After the story of the two monks, Rolf Potts has this paragraph in his book, on page 12:

"Most of us, of course, have never taken such vows - but we choose to live like monks anyway, rooting ourselves to a home or a career and using the future as a kind of phony ritual that justifies the present. In this way, we end up spending (as Thoreau put it) "the best part of one's life earning money in order to enjoy a questionable liberty during the least valuable part of it." We'd love to drop all and explore the world outside, we tell ourselves, but the time never seems right. Thus, given an unlimited amount of choices, we make none. Settling into our lives, we get so obsessed with holding on to our domestic certainties that we forget why we desired them in the first place."

This article isn't a call for you to get up a buy a couple real estate investing programs and to then quit you job.

I know many people who have pulled away from the "hand that feeds them" too early and destroyed their self confidence, because their "investing career" didn't produce buckets of cash as quickly as anticipated.

This is a reminder that there are other people like you out here. Other people who want to break their self-imposed shackles. And some that have gone ahead of you and done it.

You are not alone.

Keep reading, keep saving, keep investing, keep building, keep studying those real estate investing programs.

It may seem like slow progress at first, but each little step you take towards personal independence will pay off.

Stay focused. Stay disciplined. Don't get frustrated and give up - it's too easy to do that.

And one day, you'll wake up realizing that all those little steps have taken you to an entirely new world. One where you're the boss.

It's like getting a travel visa to a new world.

And then you can leave Communist Corporate Canada for good :-)

Until next time ... be a Renegade!

45
Let's End the Whole "Knowledge is Power" Debate

Dan Kennedy has this great line he uses:

"People very often fail despite making themselves huge repositories of knowledge. People rarely fail due to the habit of taking action on knowledge."

Have you ever noticed that some people just "know-it-all"?

They know everything about real estate investing. They know about rentals, they know about joint ventures, they know about lease/options and sandwich lease/options and they know about commercial financing and reverse mortgages and cap rates and CMHC fees and this and that and the next.

There's also an interesting observation we've made about that type of person.

They get distracted easily.

They're often the first to dismiss a talk or presentation because, "they already know about that".

But yet, they are also the people who accomplish very little.

Let me share a story.

We know a very successful real estate investor. Net worth in the tens of millions. Has his own private Jet…you know the type. He has property all over the place.

Well, don't we find him sitting in a marketing seminar we were taking a few months back? Just a few feet away from us. Blending right in with everyone else.

He's an older gentleman and was definitely older than most people in attendance.

But that didn't seem to bother him at all.

And then we learn this:

At one of the breaks, he had taken what was just learned in the seminar and was calling his staff back home to have them begin implementing what was just taught.

Literally, his time from knowledge to action was under one hour.

How instructive is that?

Here's a guy who is worth tens of millions of dollars - and yet he's investing in furthering his education and then he's implementing what he's learning immediately.

"People very often fail despite making themselves huge repositories of knowledge. People rarely fail due to the habit of taking action on knowledge."

We're often asked by friends why we continue to fly around attending different business and mastermind meetings, marketing seminars and real estate meetings

And here's the answer:

We evaluate these meetings and seminars, which cost both a fair amount of money and time, on several different levels.

The value isn't the information alone.

The real value comes from the repeated exposure to the information. This repeated, constant exposure breaks down our conscious mind's predisposition to guarding against anything "new" and "different".

Hearing about a new real estate investing tactic, or a new marketing strategy, or a new business-building technique one time is not enough.

We need repeated exposure until we are propelled into action.

It's like a battle against ourselves that we're fighting.

We understand that, although we may "know" something, we may not yet be "acting" on it.

There's a big difference.

And there's something else...

We attend these different events and meetings for one more thing.

It's for the inspirational value they provide along with the information.

You see, we've learned that if we can find sources of good knowledge and combine that with motivation and inspiration, it really accelerates our action and our results.

Knowledge alone is not enough -- you need to be pushed and prodded into action.

So although you may already "know" something, until your start "acting" on it, you need to put yourself in positions to keep hearing that information.

And you need to be surrounded by people, emails, newsletters, events and mastermind groups that inspire you into action.

So don't wander around looking for the next new thing. This is a waste of time. Trust us on that one - we know!

It's too easy to get bored. That's why most people do nothing.

Surround yourself with environments that share knowledge and inspire you. Read emails that inspire and educate. Study books, articles, newsletters that share knowledge and motivate. Hang out with action takers and before long, you'll be an action taker yourself.

Keep mixing these things together until you take action.

None of this comes from learning about something one time.

Taking action is what produces results. Knowledge alone is never enough.

I'm sure we all remember an old teacher, friend or aunt that knew almost everything about anything - but hadn't really accomplished very much at all.

Remember...

"People very often fail despite making themselves huge repositories of knowledge. People rarely fail due to the habit of taking action on knowledge."

- Dan Kennedy

Until next time...be a Renegade!

Special Free Gift #1 from the Authors
FREE Real Estate Investing Articles, Tips, Opinions…

 ☐ Yes, I want to learn as much as possible about Real Estate investing! $197 Value.

VISIT:

www.RenegadeRealEstateNewsletter.com

To sign up for a courtesy subscription to the author's "Renegade Real Estate Investing Newsletter". Just some of the topics include:

- **How to find** properties right here in Canada that make you money
- What you should know about **"buying into demand"** versus "speculating" or "flipping"
- The **most common mistakes** all beginner investors make!
- Real Estate investment tips about investment mortgages and the **latest developments** in the Canadian mortgage markets.
- How to build a **network of professionals** that will watch your back
- How to easily **increase demand** for any of your investments
- Why "systems" are more important than **any other** tips and why they are almost always overlooked

Special Gift #2 from the Authors

Copy this Page and Fax this Form to: 416-981-3467
or visit
www.YourRockStarLife.com/OneDollar.html

$1 Rock Star Inner Circle Membership

Test Drive 1 Month of Tom & Nick Karadza's Rock Star Inner Circle Membership
Receive a steady stream of investing advice

✓ Yes, I want to lock up a trial membership in your Rock Star Inner Circle. which includes:

1. ROCK STAR INNER CIRCLE WEEKLY REPORTS
2. ROCK STAR INNER CIRCLE BONUS REPORTS
3. BONUS AUDIO INTERVIEWS WITH INVESTMENT PROFESSIONALS
4. ACCESS TO PHONE IN CONSULTATIONS
5. CURRENT DAY AGREEMENTS TOM & NICK USE FOR THEIR REAL ESTATE INVESTMENTS

You have no obligation to continue at the lowest Member price of $27.00 per month. In fact, should you continue with membership, you can cancel at any time by calling The Inner Circle office at 416-848-6293 or faxing a cancellation note to 416-981-3467.] Remember, your credit card will NOT be charged the low monthly $27.00 until the 1st of the 2nd month, which means you can read, test, and **profit from all of the powerful techniques and strategies you get from being a Rock Star Inner Circle Member. And of course, it's impossible for you to lose, because if you don't absolutely LOVE everything you get, you can simply cancel your membership before the end of the month and we will even refund the $1 you paid.**

Name _____ Business Name _____

Address _____ City _____

Province_____ Postal Code_____ E-mail _____

Phone _____ Fax _____

Credit Card: ___American Express ___Visa ___MasterCard

Credit Card No. _____ Exp. Date_____

Signature _____ Date_____

Special Free Gift #3 from the Authors

FREE Copy of "Income For Life for Canadians"

Visit

www.FreeCanadianRealEstateBook.com

This book currently sells for 24.95 on Amazon.com. But you are entitled to a complete digital copy at no charge by visiting the site above.

In this book we share the details of some profitable investment strategies that have bee used to successfully invest in hundreds of investment properties across Canada.

The authors of this book can be contacted regarding other information, products, or services at the following addresses:

Tom Karadza & Nick Karadza
1011 Upper Middle Road East
Suite 1467
Oakville, Ontario, L6H 5Z9
Phone: 416-848-6293 Fax: 416-981-3467

Visit:
www.TheRealEstateRenegades.com
For articles, tips, opinions, and a
FREE Weekly Real Estate Investing Newsletter or visit
www.RenegadeRealEstateBlog.com
to access their video blog.

About the Authors

Tom Karadza quit his job as a Software Sales Manager at NetSuite Inc. as it was going public on the New York Stock Exchange (NYSE), to be a full time real estate entrepreneur and investor.

Nick Karadza also quit his job at a Fortune 500 software company, Oracle Corporation, to give real estate 100% of his focus. He began investing at the age of 21 by successfully buying, renovating, and selling a home for profit in only 3 months.

Tom and Nick Karadza are real estate professionals that are intensely focused on helping real estate investors 'on the streets'. They specialize in implementing investment systems to maximize profit in the real world. Tom and Nick have been featured in national newspapers, magazines, and television interviews such as the National Post, Canadian real Estate Magazine, Business News Network, etc.

They are active real estate investors and in 2008 they launched Rock Star Real Estate Inc., a Canadian real estate brokerage that focuses exclusively on real estate investments. They have worked with hundreds of real estate investors across Canada to implement these profitable investing strategies across southern Ontario.